Your Time To Shine!

Your Story Is Important.
Step Out From The Crowd.
Write And Publish Your Book Today.

STEVE BUELOW

New Media Jet, LLC

United States of America

This book is dedicated to the reader of *your* book,

to that one individual

whose heart *you* will touch,

whose dream *you* will inspire,

whose success *you* will encourage,

and whose life will *never* be the same.

Contents

Introduction: This Is Your Time To Shine 7

Part 1: Inspiration 21

    Chapter 1: You Can Change The World 23

    Chapter 2: Your Readers Are Waiting 49

    Chapter 3: Technology Makes It Easy 71

Part 2: Organization 101

    Chapter 4: Organized To Create 103

    Chapter 5: Organized To Connect 127

Part 3: Motivation 153

    Chapter 6: Influence And Credibility 155

    Chapter 7: Time And Financial Freedom 177

    Chapter 8: Making A Difference For Others 203

Epilogue: The Time Is Right, Now 227

Notes: Thoughts, Credits, And Links 235

The Author 241

This Is Your Time To Shine

"If you can dream it, you can do it."
- Walt Disney

I t's a conversation that seems to be repeating itself more and more frequently.

Last week, I was chatting on the phone with a new acquaintance – a friend of a friend sort of thing – and it happened again. We had been introduced through e-mail by one of my business partners, and had become Facebook friends. We also traded a number of text messages recently, and it appeared that there was genuine potential to work together on one or more of the projects in which I'm involved.

As we spoke, I could sense her passion for health and wellness, and it quickly became apparent that she possessed a significant amount of training, experience, and education.

I asked about her history – where she grew up, who were her early mentors, what were the factors that led to the decisions that she had made. I asked about her commitment and values – what drove her to turn those decisions into actions, and her dreams into her present reality. And I asked about her vision – where was the path leading, who was she bringing with her, and how they would be better off. Her answers were deep and engaging – she knows her stuff.

The longer we spoke, the more I wanted to know what *she* knew. So I asked another question, "Have you *ever* considered writing a book?"

"That is *so* interesting you asked," she said. "Yes, the name of my book is..."

She went on to describe her purpose for her book, as well as the storyline, the players, the lessons, and the outcomes that she wanted her reader to receive.

This is fantastic, I thought!

"Where can I get it? I'll buy it yet today!"

Suddenly, you could have heard a pin drop – complete silence. And then she quietly offered, "That's just it... it's all just still in my head. I've been thinking about it for years."

She confided that she had spent well more than a decade gaining the knowledge, working out her material, and formulating her plan.

At the same time, she said, she still questioned her own authority, battled too many fears, and faced multiple unknowns regarding the writing and publishing process. Taken together, these factors had combined to lock her in place, and kept her from moving forward.

"I can't believe I haven't just done it," she said. "I *so* want to make this happen. Can you help me?"

The simple answer is, yes.

Yes I can. And if *you* have ever experienced similar thoughts or fears, take heart. I can help you too. In fact, I've been waiting for you. I wrote this book just *for* you – and about you.

About your hopes, your dreams, your desires to get your thoughts and feelings out and to get your awesome work written and published – right now.

That is what I believe you deserve, and with today's technology, it's never been easier or more affordable to do.

It's true.

Technology has changed our industry dramatically, and with those changes created more opportunities for more people than at any other time in history. The question, of course, is whether you know how to *use* that technology... how to harness the tremendous power of the new tools... to get done what you want to get done.

To complete your book. To publish and sell your book. To gain the recognition, respect, and rewards you deserve. To have control over your time and finances. To live the life you want to live – where you want to live. To invest your time and resources doing the things you really want to do, with the people whom you love and care about most.

Oh yes – and to change a significant piece of the world in the process.

What an awesome time to be alive!

I was thinking the other day about all of the wonderful benefits of this new technology. How it has changed so much about the way we live and how we work. How we use it to expand our interests, meet people, and connect with one another.

And suddenly it occurred to me that it is entirely possible that the best friend that either of us may *ever* have could be someone whom we haven't even met yet. And the same could be said for what may become our favorite restaurant in a town we've never visited, the perfect vacation spot, or the ideal church for ourselves and our family – all these wonderful little gifts that wind their way through our lives. Terrific surprises that simply seem to show up.

But it goes deeper than that.

You see, I believe that *you* are one of those gifts. I believe that *you* are one of those wonderful surprises that will one day show up in the life of someone whom you have yet to meet. Yes, I believe that your work, your passion, your feelings, your art, your book may inspire something as big as a movement, or as important as influencing, improving or saving an individual life.

In fact, I believe that one of the reasons that you are reading these words today is because there are all these little pieces of you that the world is just longing to get to know.

Further, I think there are hundreds – maybe even thousands – of people whose lives would be just a little better off, a little less stressful, a little more enjoyable, if only they knew you. If they knew your thoughts, if they learned from your experience, if they understood your feelings and hopes and dreams.

You are a writer!

You may write for many different reasons. Maybe you write to inspire. Maybe you write to uplift and encourage. Maybe you write to entertain or to teach or to heal. Regardless, as you write your stories, your words impact others.

There are just one or two challenges.

Either your book hasn't been pulled together and completed yet, or... it hasn't been published yet.

So right this very minute, people are online and they're searching for inspiration and searching for answers and searching for solutions, but they can't find you. Today millions of people will go to Barnes & Noble and they'll log on to Amazon and... you're not there.

That is a conversation that I believe you and I deserve to have, because both of those situations – the writing and publishing of your work – are resolved more easily today than you've likely ever imagined.

And that is the reason I wrote this book.

It is also the reason my daughter and I founded our publishing company, New Media Jet, and the reason that we produced a *step-by-step* video class that not only guarantees you can be published and in major outlets within as little as 30 days, but also gives you everything you need to get into the publishing business for yourself – as in, for profit.

Yes, you... writer *and* publisher.

This means that once you learn the process, you will never have to ask for a publisher's permission again – ever.

Please know that I have a passion to see your work completed and published:

1) At the right price – something that anyone can afford, that fits into every budget.
2) With the right royalties – money in your purse, wallet, or bank account.
3) In the right places – your works available online at Barnes & Noble, Amazon, and other quality national booksellers.
4) At the right time – as in, right now.

If you've dabbled with this idea before, if you've ever tried or even considered taking on the project of getting your book written and to market, you know what a terribly complicated process that has been in the past.

In fact, for much of the last five centuries, you could have spent your entire life in an attempt to persuade, convince, or cajole a publisher to print and distribute your book – and still never have seen your dream come true.

I can't even imagine the volumes of wisdom, insight, and innovation that have been buried along with their creators because they didn't happen to fit a publishing giant's current business model, publishing calendar, or marketing plan.

Well, what a difference a few years and some silicon chips can make! And welcome to the revolution – you're about to be pleasantly surprised.

Thank Goodness For Change

The year was 1992, and a large, white envelope had just been delivered to my office by priority mail, along with a request for delivery confirmation. Weighing just over 2.4 pounds and addressed to me, it contained 228 pages of double-spaced text bound simply and neatly in a black vinyl report cover – the first book manuscript made to publisher's specifications that I had ever seen.

A small, yellow post-it note accompanied the package, with the author's handwritten instructions to, "Read Chapters V, VI and VIII after XI."

The goal was straightforward enough – he hoped I could help him find a way to get his book published.

Started in 1961, it had been 31 years in the making and, like wine, had been perfected with each passing year. Though a heady political-science work, so well thought-through were its principles that few could argue with its reasoning or conclusions, regardless of which side of the political spectrum the reader was on.

The sender happened to be an attorney – one of *my* attorneys – a gentleman who at 55 years of age was at the very top of his game.

Working in the high-pressure world of corporate mergers and acquisitions for a not-for-profit health care system in the Chicago area, he nevertheless called rural Wisconsin his home, living just over the border with his wife of forever in an elegant and peaceful retreat they designed together – and for each other.

I often made the two and a half hour trip to their home to discuss business matters, and over time our relationship grew beyond that of merely attorney-client. I respected his insights, integrity, and experience – he respected my marketing ability, perseverance, and energy. We knew that eventually we'd find a way to work together, and maybe his new book would be the place to start.

At the time, I was serving as President and CEO of an established and growing HR Consulting company that I had founded with several partners five years earlier, and was also involved in several start-up ventures in niche markets that complemented our primary services nicely.

Further, I had just recently begun to ponder what an impact could be made, and what doors could be opened, if one were not only *willing* to write – but were also *able* to get published. And therein lay the challenge – willing and able.

Those were the days when a handful of powerful editors at very large companies could make or break a career, and that's exactly what they did. It was a very different time for the publishing world in general, and for authors and aspiring authors in particular.

In fact, another 20 years would pass before my attorney would see his dream of having his book published become a reality – until I shared with him the convergence of tools and technology that radically altered the writing and publishing world forever. Just in time for him... and for you.

Something In Common

As I tell the above story – and I often do – a funny thing happens. People learn about one individual's commitment, desire, and passion to add his or her ideas to the discussion – or to start an entirely new conversation altogether.

They hear about the struggle, the challenges, and the rejection that others have gone through on the way to getting their books organized, written, published, and into the hands of the marketplace through major outlets like Amazon or Barnes & Noble.

They see the amazing level of influence and credibility that comes with writing and publishing one's first book, and how simple it is to expand those qualities further by writing and publishing subsequent works. And they want it for themselves. I get this type of feedback all the time:

"Steve, I've never told you, but I have a book in me... I've always believed that!"

"I *am* that person... the one who was always going to write a book!"

"Everyone says I should write a book about this subject... I've certainly lived it!"

"I've journaled for years... my writings could fill volumes!"

Sound familiar?

More than likely it does, or you wouldn't be researching and reading a book on how to write and become a published author. And your timing couldn't be better.

Oh, how things have changed!

Only a few short years ago, I had just co-authored a

book for a counselor in the health care field and the next step was the monumental task of getting publishers to look at it.

Amazingly, after just a few contacts we began to have several positive responses to our work.

If you've ever diligently searched out scores of publishers and carefully mailed untold manuscripts according to their specifications, you know how uncommon this is. You have also likely experienced how the exhilaration and anticipation of your early efforts can turn to disappointment upon reading one rejection letter after another.

So imagine how we felt when there was strong initial interest. We were flat-out fired up! Unfortunately, a wake up call was right behind. You see, the days of the big advances and publisher's promotional packages were gone.

Yes, we were told, they'd publish our book... we'd just need to come up with a tidy sum of somewhere between $45-$60,000 for publishing costs, minimum printing runs, and marketing materials and campaigns.

It had sounded *so* good up to that point.

I knew there had to be a better way and became determined to find it. Yes, I would find it for my friends, for my clients, for my family, for myself, and for you – for all the authors in my life who have dreamed about this day for years.

Nothing To Wait For

As you read these pages – as you begin to learn and grow and dream again – one thing is going to become abundantly clear. There is no need to wait anymore. It's time for the world to find out who you are.

You are a person of influence, a trusted confidante, a creator and teller of stories – a writer. And you want to get your stories into the hands of readers.

Now, here's the good news – as you read this, everything has lined up to make your dreams and vision a reality.

By reading and understanding the principles in *Your Time To Shine*, you are quickly going to realize that you *do* have the power to change your circumstances, and those of others – that you *can* do this.

In Part 1, you will be inspired to see that not only has life already prepared you for this endeavor, it has also assembled your audience, and created technology that now stands ready to bring you and your audience together – today.

In Part 2, you will be given guidelines, tips, and plans to get organized to save you time, energy, frustration, and expense in pulling together and assembling your work, and also in connecting with your market both before and after your book's completion.

Finally, in Part 3, you will be motivated to move toward the life you desire – to be recognized as an expert in your chosen subject or genre, to receive the financial rewards and the freedom of time you deserve, and to share a legacy of success, hope, understanding, and healing with countless others in this and future generations to follow. But we have to get started.

"I just picked up your new book," a friend told me recently. "I love reading your work! And I can't help thinking that I should be writing too... I know it would be good for my business. I *think* about it all the time!"

"I agree completely," I said, "but we both know that

thinking about it isn't how it gets done. What's holding you back, and would you like some help?"

My friend then related two of his biggest concerns – two concerns that are faced by nearly *everyone* who dreams about writing and publishing:

1) Will anyone read it?

2) What should it be about?

Now, it may not surprise you that I think everyone ought to be writing – whether they have an audience to read it or not. Writing crystallizes our thinking… hones our arguments… and solidifies our points of view.

Writing expands our world, and brings clarity to our beliefs and our hopes and our dreams. It allows us to work out our challenges – and to share our victories and our losses… our pleasures and our pain.

It connects us with others who have the same joys, feelings, priorities, and fears. And it allows us to work out practically what we've only previously thought about mentally or emotionally.

Even if no one ever picks up your manuscript, reads your article, or clicks on your content, you are still better off for writing. Period.

But then again, that's really not how it works. You may start alone, but you won't be alone for long. I told my friend with absolute certainty that he would most definitely have readers for his book.

How could I promise such a thing?

"Well, first of all," I said, smiling, "I will be reading it, and, last time I checked, I am someone. Further, if you're really nice… I bet that one day, we could even interest your wife and kids!"

Of course, that's just the start. As unique as you are, your thoughts and experiences are, nevertheless, shared by many others... in fact, probably millions.

And as you write – as you speak from the heart – you will attract others to you who feel and think the exact same way. And there's no pressure – no need for pretense – for by now you understand that the days of trying to be all things to all people are gone... hopefully forever. Life and love and business and impact are about relationships with people. And great relationships are built on strong foundations of common values and experience.

So as we write, we connect. As we write, we give. Then we write and connect and give some more. And as our seeds are planted, we know that one day the benefits that others have enjoyed through our work and our writing will return to us as well.

Eventually, on this earth... planting time leads to harvest time – every time.

Okay, so what about concern number two – what should my friend write about? More importantly, what should *you* write about?

It really is a simple matter, I told him.

"After all," I explained, "you're not writing for *The New York Times*. Thank God, you're not writing for *The New York Times*!! On the contrary, you are going to write something that people are actually interested in reading!"

Need proof? Find something in America that is falling farther and faster than newspaper circulation and subscription rates.

But alas, I digress.

We live in a world of information and ideas, where technology has brought us all just a little closer together, able to reach out to help and impact and influence both people and situations that were impossibly remote just a few short years ago.

"There's just one little thing missing," I told David, "and that's your perspective. We need your ideas – and then we'll be complete!"

Okay, I know – that wasn't really true. Getting David's ideas won't make us complete.

No, in fact, that won't happen until we get *your* ideas!

Yes, we need your book, and producing the content really isn't that difficult. In fact, discovering what to write is as simple as discovering a little bit of yourself.

You see, I believe that your book is already written.

Try this for starters.

Take any issue that matters to you, and honestly communicate your thoughts on how to improve it. That's it – fix something – and then tell the rest of us how you did it.

Or how about this?

Share a story. Provide expertise. Increase the knowledge base. Or promote your causes. Leave a legacy. Add value.

Tell us your hopes, your dreams, your fears and your failures. Use your words to inspire our youth, encourage our weak, honor our warriors, and respect our elderly. Lift up the broken, teach the willing, and reinforce core values.

Yes, please tell us what brings laughter to your soul – or tears to your eyes. What is important to you – and why?

For *whom* do you live – and for *what* would you die?

Part 1
Inspiration

Chapter 1
You Can Change The World

"I want to do it because I want to do it."
- Amelia Earhart

Growing up, I always knew that someday I was going to do something really special.

And while I never knew the form it would take, I believed that whatever I did would positively influence a ton of people and cause a great amount of happiness, stability, and prosperity for all those it touched.

I also figured that somehow it would likely result in major career advantages for me, but I must admit, that part of the plan was always a bit fuzzy.

You see, I never really knew what I wanted to do.

When I was a kid, I remember that some adults – in particular, a number of teachers and a well-meaning extended relative or two – often told me that I was "nothing but a dreamer."

It usually started this way:

Them: "So, Steve… what are you going to be when you grow up?"

Me: "Oh, I don't know. I don't want much… I only want to change the world."

After which, it generally ended this way:

Them: "You are *such* a dreamer. You know, one day you're going to need to get *real serious* about getting a job somewhere."

Me: "Yes… I remember that from what you told me last time, thanks."

Now, please understand, from my perspective, there were at least two points that were glaringly wrong with this argument:

1) I started my first real business for pay while still in grade school, and had several more in high school. From the time I was about eight years old, I never thought much about working my way up someone else's ladder, figuring instead that, one way or another, we'd find a way to make it on our own – in our own business.

2) All this talk of real serious job-getting tended to come from the same people who told me that I could be whatever I wanted when I grew up. This was, after all, America.

Yes, it seemed, I could do anything – I could *be* anything – just as long as the "anything" fit neatly within their comfort zone. The pressure continued to mount over the next few years, culminating with a date in my high school guidance counselor's office around January of my senior year. What happened next is important, but first allow me to digress for just a moment.

I'd like to ask you a question that may get at the root cause behind why your awesome book is not yet completed and published, and why, when you are asked what you do for a living, you don't enthusiastically tell people that, "I'm an author! I write and publish books that help people do *x!*"

Here is my question: what would you think if I suddenly told you that from this point forward in your life, you had to allow a seventeen year old to choose the path you will follow for the remainder of your career?

Good idea or bad idea?

That's right. You agree to let this young man or woman, with no experience whatsoever and consulting only a high school guidance counselor, to decide what, if any, further education you'll receive, and in which industry and occupation you'll spend the rest of your working life.

Let me ask again... good idea or bad idea? Do I hear, "That's ridiculous! Who on earth would agree to that?"

Well, it seems, just about everyone. Because that's pretty much what each of us was asked to do when we hit that precious age of seventeen – make a career choice as to where we were going to spend a good part of the next forty-five or fifty-five years. You likely did it – so did I.

Now back to my appointment with Mr. Lifepath, our school's guidance counselor – it was Decision Day. Out came the book of careers and colleges, trades and trade schools. And advice... lots of advice.

"Well Steve, with these grades you *really* need to go to college. You could be a teacher or an engineer. Maybe get involved in a management or executive track. What do you think you'd *really* like to do?"

With all due respect, I was a seventeen year old boy! The things that I *really* liked to do didn't pay any money, and they also risked getting me in *a lot* of trouble with my mom!

So that night, I got together with my friend, Pat, and we came up with a plan. We decided it would be a good idea to apply to the Pre-Med Program at Marquette University, and one day, we would open a dental practice together. I remember this made my family very proud, mainly because we didn't share with them our rationale.

You see, Pat and I had run the numbers and figured out (remember, we were seventeen) that any dentist worth his salt could make enough in one day a week, to golf the next four in a row. And then we could take the weekend off.

Yes, that seemed like a very good plan at the time – a very good plan, indeed. Though, as I think back to that "Decision Day," it is apparent that three career paths were conspicuously missing from the choices I was given:

1) Small Business Owner.

2) Thought Leader and Author.

3) High School Guidance Counselor.

The irony of point number three didn't hit me until years later... if he was so up on the best career choices, why was he not doing one of them?

As it turned out, I ended up picking the first one and have been happily self-employed for most of my adult life. Interestingly, that path also required me to invest a great deal of time thinking and writing, and along the way, I even became a darn good teacher.

Imagine that.

And I think it was this desire to stay outside the traditional employment lines that pushed me to take a few risks and to question the wisdom of that seventeen-year-old, a decision which ultimately allowed me to find myself today doing something that is really special – writing words of inspiration daily, producing ideas that transform, sowing seeds of knowledge and encouragement into you as an aspiring author, and giving you both the tools and the permission to change the path you're on and begin to live the life you desire and were meant to live!

I often wonder why more people don't choose to step out on their own and follow their inner voice – the dream within. Those who know me well know that from time to time I like to conduct my own informal studies just to get the flavor of what's going on in the minds of average people as they're just going about their day. What are they thinking? What are their concerns? What keeps them up at night with either joy or grief – anticipation or anxiety?

And just to be clear, let me start by acknowledging that in terms of a truly scientific study… this method would fail miserably. That is, of course, unless scientific studies involved grabbing a handful of random people… asking them one question… and then extrapolating the results across the entire population and publishing my results!

But it is interesting to me anyway, and, for that reason alone, that's just how I do things once in a while!

Here is what I did recently. Every day for about a week or so, I presented this question to at least one person – some days, more – and then I tracked the results. Actually, tracking the results was quite easy, because I received exactly the same answer from everyone!

Here was the question: "If you had the choice, would you rather do what you're doing now for your current employer; or would you rather be working for yourself in a similar capacity or another field of your choosing?"

That's it. If you had the choice, would you rather work for yourself or someone else?

Ready for the surprise results? 100% of the respondents said that if they had the choice, they would absolutely work for themselves. And that is what I find so amazing. Remember, this is America. Since when *haven't* they had the choice, and just whom are they expecting to give it to them?

Study after study after study shows that nearly two out of every three Americans feel unfulfilled by their work and underappreciated in their workplace. Four out of five would leave their jobs with little notice if they won a lottery jackpot.

Many are disheartened, disappointed, and disillusioned. Most believe they are overworked and underpaid. The majority admit they would do something else if they felt they could afford it. Some would prefer to simply volunteer and give their lives to altruistic endeavors. Many more would start their own businesses if they believed they could manage the financial risk.

Yes, and countless others like you and me would begin living their passion, sharing their experiences with others, writing and producing and publishing and teaching, if only they knew three simple processes – just three simple things:

1) How to use the new tools to make their move with virtually no cost.
2) How to achieve significant financial success using only their spare time.
3) How to create the life of their dreams without risking their current income.

I was fortunate. I realized early that the decisions I made at seventeen were not necessarily in my long-term best interests. I was already in the free-enterprise economy and therefore attuned to the changes that were going on in the market and in technology. I was heavily engaged within the human resources and employment sectors and saw the challenges faced by genuinely good people on a daily basis – how those challenges devastated marriages and families and broke up relationships.

I could see that I wasn't getting younger and that if I didn't start living my dream now that there was no guarantee that it would ever happen at all – but what about you?

What if you've reached a point in your journey after ten or twelve years – or even twenty or thirty years – where you suspect the seventeen year old was wrong?

If you've given it your all, and there's something still missing, it may be time to change course. If you've always wanted to write – if you feel compelled to publish, to influence others – there has never been an easier time to begin living your dream.

There has never been a better time to start leading – to start writing. Over twenty-seven million of your neighbors and fellow citizens have stepped away from the job world either part-time or full-time to pursue their vision of having some freedom for themselves.

And there is plenty of room for one more – for you.

The Best Thing That Ever Happened

Several months ago, I had the opportunity to speak with an individual who was, to use his words, totally stressed out. Anxiety, pressure, fear, insomnia, and anger… all were mentioned inside of twenty minutes.

Oh, yes – *freaked out* was in there too.

It seems the economy was threatening his job and that was threatening his finances which then threatened his attitude which spilled over and threatened his relationships and that was now threatening his health.

I suggested he stop the threats.

I spend a ton of time writing and teaching about fixing what's not working. The first step is always an honest evaluation of the current situation, and its relationship to reaching concrete goals in a specific time period.

The questions are really pretty simple. Where am I now and where am I headed? If I stay on the current path, will I reach the objectives I set for the end of this quarter, next quarter, end of the year, etc.?

What do I need to change to stay on course? It works in every area of our lives, from our relationships to finances to physical health to spiritual growth – you name it.

The economy isn't the problem – not adjusting to meet changing circumstances, is. As the leaders of our own lives, we accept the responsibility of running the race, and getting to the destination, in spite of the obstacles.

And the quickest way I know to get the focus off of ourselves and our challenges is to, well… get the focus off of ourselves and our challenges – to focus on helping someone else.

This also just happens to be the perfect job description for you or me or anyone that would like to begin writing and publishing work that actually sells!

And the beauty is that when we find a way to help relieve the stress, anxiety, pressure, and fear that someone else is feeling… our stress, anxiety, pressure, and fear seems to just magically fade away.

Truth is, it's not magic – it's life.

So, back to the gentleman I mentioned a minute ago. I asked him if he was any good at what he did for a living. Sticking out his chest, he suggested that he was one of the best.

So I asked what they paid him per hour. "$23.50," came the response. "And what do they bill you out at?" I asked. "$90-$130 an hour, depending on the client."

I suggested that losing that particular job might be the best thing that ever happened to him... that he was worth up to one hundred dollars an hour more to his clients than he was to his employer.

That realization has launched a million dreams!

Then I asked one other question to solidify his thinking. "If you had the power, what one thing would you share with others that would make their lives simpler or easier or better – maybe something so over-the-top cool or innovative, so extraordinary or meaningful or remarkable that you'd be remembered long after you're gone?"

"Steve, I have *so many* ideas... there are things I know and experiences I've had that could help *so many* people," he said. "I have a whole series of books, just on my hobbies alone. Will you help me?"

Bingo! Major transformation!

Desperation replaced by hope, fear destroyed by excitement, depression swallowed up by purpose, and a kinder, gentler, more respectful attitude in all his personal and professional relationships.

And wouldn't you know it – I hear his health is improving and he's been sleeping better as well.

Embrace The Real You

Often as we go through life, the challenges we face on the outside are quite manageable when contrasted with those we face on the inside.

As a leader – as a soon-to-be-published author – you need to be aware of the most common obstacles and pitfalls that can keep you from soaring. At times, these may take the form of negative emotions such as fear, anger, resentment, blame, guilt, disappointment, etc.

Most often, however, the chains that hold you back from living the life that you desire and deserve are hidden in plain view in the form of ideas, beliefs, and expectations – both your own and those of others.

So here's a question: do you know how amazing you really are?

Before you answer, let me say in no uncertain terms that I believe that you are perfect – and perfectly prepared – for the mission that you feel you have in front of you and for the book that you are about to write. If it weren't true, you wouldn't have the dream and you wouldn't feel the calling that burns within you this very minute.

I also believe that your life, my life, and the lives of tens of thousands of others across the world are linked by unique bonds, and if that's true, then what we do – what you do – does indeed matter.

Now, be on the lookout because it's not unusual at this point for a whole range of feelings to rise up to put the process on hold, to question your value or standing or authority to address the topic, issue, or cause you have chosen.

In fact, if taking the next step causes a slight amount of

fear, a little uneasiness or anxiety, take heart – you are exactly where you need to be.

As I travel and as I speak with new leaders and potential authors, by far the most common stumbling block occurs when people begin making comparisons between themselves and others.

While this happens to be rooted – sometimes deeply – in the image we have of ourselves, it is, nonetheless, easily defeated by our resolve to live with authenticity, an acceptance that we are good enough, and an understanding that who we are – as well as all we have done and experienced – can be a joy or blessing or lesson to someone else.

In fact, as I write – and as you are now reading – there is only one question that is absolutely dominating my thoughts: I wonder, who is it that needs to hear your story right now?

Many years ago, a mentor told me that anytime we compare ourselves to others, we lose.

The way the principle was described to me, and the way I have described it to countless others, is like this:

If I compare myself with you, all I know about you is what you have shown me.

In other words, more than likely, all I know is your absolute best characteristics. On the other hand, in my mind, I know all of my own worst traits, because, well… I've lived them!

So, now I take all of your best qualities, and I compare them against all of my own worst failings, and voila – I have, in effect, widened the gap to the furthest possible extent!

Not wise.

Your goal is to become completely comfortable with yourself – with the real, genuine, authentic you. Let's look for a moment at how this authenticity, and your acceptance of yourself and your experiences, plays out in real life – in the life of someone else.

I would like to share this story with you because it had such a profound effect on the person to whom I was speaking, and in so doing, had a similarly powerful effect on me.

This conversation revolved around the concept as it relates to being real – and being *real approachable* – to those whom we might influence as we go about our business and through our daily lives.

It all started when a young man called me for advice on a business matter. He had made some promises, had lost a significant five-figure sum, and now stood to lose even more... if he kept his word.

He wanted to know what to do.

"Well, it's really pretty simple," I said. "You just need to figure out if your word is any good or not."

Silence…

Followed by six or seven additional seconds of absolutely no talking whatsoever!

Then, he said, "Yeah, I knew that's what you were going to say, but man, you don't know how it feels to lose that kind of money."

Oh my.

I asked if he had a few extra minutes, and then described a period of great financial loss in my life – in fact, a loss many times the size we had just discussed seconds earlier. I spoke of the stress, the depression, the sleepless nights.

He was stunned – and thankful. Through sharing my story, he received the gift of hope.

Would I walk this road with him, he asked. And the answer, of course, was yes. After all, it may be part of the reason I had to learn such a difficult lesson in the first place.

Authenticity.

It means allowing others into our life and, without pretense, letting them see us as we really are, even when we're not at our best.

It is showing our humanness... and yes, sometimes even our brokenness.

Authenticity is the source of the strength and friendship that comes from shared experience, whether that means enjoying similar interests or activities, or overcoming similar situations.

It is knowing, because, well... you just know.

One of my favorite old scriptures refers to the fact that we all go through the same sort of stuff (my translation). It means that there are things in life that bond us together – that, regardless of our circumstances or upbringing, we're not *that* different.

Now, I need to make an important distinction.

The story above was pretty heavy, and represented some fairly negative circumstances for me personally. In a split second, I had to decide whether to allow this gentleman to see the hurts, the challenges, the pain, and the failure of previous decisions. I had to resist putting on a perfect face, and I had to be open to allowing him to see me fall.

But it was the only way I could help him – the only way he could relate to me.

Only by seeing my fall could he also witness my will to get back up again and again and again. And only by gaining his trust and respect could I have walked him and his family to the other side of the minefield, through the fire I had seen several times before.

But don't misunderstand. Authenticity is not about being heavy and dark – it's simply about being real. It's about knowing yourself first, and attracting your market second – a subject we will cover in significantly greater depth in the next chapter.

You Can Do This

I've recently had a number of conversations with people who have been struggling, and it would seem that a large part of that struggle is the picture they see of themselves, and the words they use to describe themselves, when they're all alone.

Yes, it's a real-life big-time identity crisis – and it's nothing new.

I am reminded of a number of stories going all the way back to Biblical times where it was so important for people to chart a new course that they literally had to take on a complete change in identity. And, wouldn't you know it, as part of that identity change, they were actually given a whole new name.

So Abram and Sarai became Abraham and Sarah... subtle changes that represented an entirely different mindset.

Look it up.

Likewise, Jacob became Israel... Simon became Peter... Saul became Paul... and a ton of others with names you can barely pronounce.

Don't believe me?

Try Belteshazzar or Zaphenath-Paneah or Meshach, for example... but alas, I digress.

The point is that what we believe about ourselves – indeed, what we *see* and what we *say* about ourselves – can have a profound effect upon our outcomes. Sure, what others do and say can influence us if we allow it, but *our own* thoughts and *our own* beliefs and *our own* words can make or break us quickly.

Henry Ford once said, "Whether you think you can or think you can't, you're right." And he was right on the money. For sure, if you believe the negative – if you believe you *can't* – the chances of success are limited.

Are you persuasive?

A people person?

Good with money or relationships or the opposite sex?

Are you full of life and energy and vitality and strength?

Are you good with math or other subjects?

How about an excellent cook?

A good reader, teacher, listener, writer, storyteller, poet, parent, or artist?

Are you superior at any crafts, hobbies, sports, or vocations?

Could you be?

If your answer is negative – if you reject the ability to improve – there is little hope to achieve in those areas. And the reason is simple. If we claim despair and frustration and hopelessness – if we believe that we can't – then what is the use of even trying? It becomes a self-fulfilling prophecy.

On the other hand, if we can change our words, we can change our thoughts and beliefs. If we can change our thoughts and beliefs, we can change our expectations. If we can change our expectations, we can change our actions. And when we change our actions, we change our position in life and our identity.

First, we change how we see ourselves, *then* we change how the rest of the world sees us as well.

Your Best Is Good Enough

From time to time, we have all heard coaches, trainers, teachers, and consultants give the well-worn and generally-accepted advice that in order to really succeed, you must devote 110% of yourself and your efforts to whatever it is that you are doing. Every time I run into this comment, I always wonder about the magic of that number. After all, if someone *could actually* give 110%, why not demand more?

Make it 112%, 120%, 137%!

The truth is, you can't do it... nor do you need to.

Should you focus your attention? *Yes.*

Assemble a team to help you? *Without a doubt.*

Hone the skills required to accomplish your vision? *Absolutely.*

Work yourself to an early grave at the expense of your relationships? *Ridiculous.*

Now, I was no math major, but I do know this – if I give you all of whatever I have, I have given you 100%, no more, no less. It is all that there is.

And if I invest 100% of my time or effort to one goal, activity, or endeavor, then I do it at the expense of every other important event, responsibility, and relationship in my life – and only a fool would define that as success.

Our objective should be to *do our best* with focused and positive energy – to improve and increase in efficiency and effectiveness, whenever and wherever possible.

As an aspiring author, as an up-and-coming leader, this simple formula, practiced consistently over time, will absolutely separate you from the masses, and give you the time, the freedom, the recognition, and the life you deserve.

On September 25, 2010, I wrote and published an online article in which I predicted that Clay Matthews, linebacker for the Green Bay Packers, would be named the National Football League's 2010-11 Defensive Player Of The Year when the voting took place early the following year.

As it turned out, I was wrong, and the award (by just two votes) went to Troy Polamalu of the Pittsburgh Steelers.

But Matthews and his team had the final victory – less than one week later, they would defeat Polamalu and the Steelers 31-25 in Super Bowl XLV.

Now, there's no question that I proved that my fortune-telling skills need some work, but you must admit I was close. The questions are, how and why did I make that prediction publicly at the beginning of the season many months earlier?

Obviously, Clay Matthews is good – really good. But good players in the NFL are a dime a dozen. Well, make that 200,000,000 dimes! The point is, often times good players in the NFL are just like good players in the rest of the world – they get comfortable. They get satisfied. And satisfaction with the current situation – satisfaction with being pretty good – keeps them from doing and being their best. The same is true for us, and it keeps us from reaching our true and God-given potential.

Am I saying that God has a plan for you that you might miss if you don't strive for your best and follow your dream?

Well, yes, I guess I am, though that's just my opinion.

The point is, I made my prediction about Matthews because he *is not* satisfied – and that is why he will go from good, to great.

For example, in the off-season he learned that by studying Mixed Martial Arts (MMA), he could use his talents and his body much more effectively against his opponent. So he sought out the best trainer he could find and got busy.

It is the same thing you are doing now by reading this book, and by searching for resources, tools, and people that can help you achieve your vision of getting your ideas out and your terrific work published.

We must do our best, and our best is good enough. That said, I have three questions:

1) How important is it to you to be successful as a writer?
2) How interested are you in raising the bar of your personal best?
3) How will your life be different 12 months from now if you do?

It may be as simple as learning some new technology or burying your fear of rejection or the unknown. It might require you to network more or read more or search out a mentor, trainer, or coach.

It could mean turning off the television one or two nights a week, or focusing intently on improving your health, finances, or personal or spiritual relationships. It may mean letting go of disappointments or guilt or unproductive thoughts and habits and activities in your past. And it will be absolutely life-transforming, for you – and others.

As you read this, there are countless people whose most urgent hope and prayer can *only* be answered by meeting you. It is *my* hope and prayer that you will not be satisfied until you fulfill *their* hope and prayer.

You see, it is my belief that becoming your best isn't just about personal glory and achievement. It's not all about position or power or wealth or prosperity, though it may include those elements. It isn't about temporary gain or toys or pleasure. The reason to *become* our best... is so that we can *give* our best.

Live Today

When Ron Heagy and his younger brother left to go surfing the day before Ron's eighteenth birthday, he never imagined that it would be the last time he would move anything below his neck. That was 1980.

Some time back, I met Ron. He was speaking at an event I attended and his presence on stage commanded attention. The first words out of his mouth were these:

"I had a great day today, a really great day. But I want you to know, it may be my last."

There were several hundred people in the room – and you could hear a pin drop.

"Though I have to tell you," he continued, "it could be *your* last day, too." Total silence.

"Two questions," he said. "If this is your last day, was it also your best day? And, if not... why not?"

Good questions.

Here is some additional food for thought:

The story is told of Nadine Stair, who at 85 was asked how she would live if she could do it all over again.

Among other things, she said, "I'd make more mistakes next time. I'd relax. I would limber up. I would be sillier than I have been on this trip. I would take fewer things seriously. I would take more chances. I would climb more mountains and swim more rivers. I would eat more ice cream and less beans. I would perhaps have more actual troubles, but I'd have fewer imaginary ones. You see, I'm one of those people who live sensibly and sanely hour after hour, day after day. Oh, I've had my moments, and if I had to do it over again, I'd have more of them. In fact, I'd try to have nothing else. Just moments, one after another, instead of living so many years ahead of each day. I've been one of those persons who never goes anywhere without a thermometer, a hot water bottle, and a raincoat. If I had to do it over again, I would travel lighter than I have. If I had my life to live over, I would start barefoot earlier in the spring and stay that way later in the fall. I would go to more dances. I would ride more merry-go-rounds, and pick more daisies."

My sister called me recently to tell me of a friend who she said was *really* living life right now.

"When did she start living?" I asked.

The answer was one I have heard so often.

"Well," my sister began, "about six years ago she was diagnosed with a potentially life-altering medical situation. It was very scary. She beat the disease, and determined to never sit on the sidelines again. In fact, her entire life she had always been so reserved. So... proper. She's suddenly taking the initiative. She went after a relationship that she really wanted. She remarried at sixty, and is traveling and enjoying life more than ever! She's a completely different person – it's changed everything!"

Quite likely, you also know people with similar stories. They're everywhere – people who seemingly wait to live, until it's time to die.

The truth is that there is no better time than *now* to do the things we've always wanted to do, and, to be sure, there is no guarantee that there will *be* any other time.

So, the only questions become:

1) What are we waiting for?

2) Why?

Decide To Pursue Your Dreams

I was going to start this section by giving you permission to *follow* your dreams, but that's not strong enough. I want you to *chase* them down! I want you to pursue them! Consistently, fearlessly, relentlessly – with honesty, character, and integrity!

And it all begins by making decisions about how you want your life to look, what impact you want to make, and what activities, relationships, and values are absolute and non-negotiable priorities. This process is so important because it serves to ground us on a daily basis, and provides the confident assurance that we will not be sidetracked by the never-ending stream of expectations, choices, and demands that are placed on us and our time.

This is an issue that affects everyone. Having led or participated in thousands of meetings over the years, I have often witnessed powerful business and community leaders struggle with decision-making. The same holds true for individuals who run charitable foundations, as well as those of us who must not only balance careers and families, but are also now focused on changing their path to align with their vision. It can also be true of you and me.

The challenge for most is not that we don't have enough information. Indeed, we can generally access all the knowledge and data, facts and intelligence, history, projections, advice, counsel, and forecasts in literal nanoseconds!

On the contrary, more often than not the challenge comes from not fully comprehending the big picture, the hard result, the goals and priorities that must be achieved for the organization – corporate or domestic – to fulfill its purpose on earth.

It is *all* about the mission, the dream, the purpose.

And the purpose is about the ultimate reason for being. It is about knowing, in no uncertain terms, what is singularly important; what cannot be left undone.

It's about passion and vision, and having detailed and precise answers to questions like:

1) Where are we now?
2) Where are we going?
3) Why is this important?
4) What resources are required?
5) What are the major obstacles?
6) What is the timetable?
7) Who's coming along with us, and how will they benefit?

These aren't platitudes, mind you – these are plans. You see, when our life's mission or purpose is clearly defined and understood, making decisions is simple. Each option is weighed in terms of its effect on the necessary outcome. If we proceed with this idea, does it move us toward our mission... or does it take us away? Maybe it's neutral.

So, here's how we score it.

If it moves us further away from our mission, we dismiss it out of hand. If it's neutral, we will likely dismiss it also, in favor of a more effective use for our time, energy, and resources. Such ideas and options are not necessarily bad; they just don't fit with the stated mission and map of where we are headed.

If it moves us toward our goal, we then need only to compare it with other options that also meet our criteria. Again, no options or ideas are necessarily good or bad; some simply do not provide an effective means to achieving the mission, and others do.

In his book *Winning*, former General Electric CEO Jack Welch describes the company's mission during a period of his tenure. Each GE business unit was to be "Number 1 or Number 2 in every market." Third place wasn't an option. The plan called for "fixing, selling, or closing every under-performing business that couldn't get there."

Now, they could have chosen from a thousand and one other missions, and so can you. It was simply the concrete vision that GE cast for themselves, and the unwavering commitment to the plan that was required of all the team players.

A few years ago, I received a call from a high school senior who was nearing graduation. It seems she had been accepted to Vanderbilt University and was about to set upon a path to study Veterinary Medicine.

Just one problem... she had no desire to become a veterinarian.

Excuse me?

That's right. Yet virtually her entire family was planning a huge *bon voyage* party to launch her into the rest of her life as Doctor Daughter.

Interestingly enough, the night before she called I had received a message from her mother, who had asked if I'd be willing to speak with her daughter. In fact it was the mom who first informed me that the girl was having second thoughts about her decision.

As the mother and I spoke, she confided, "This is really a problem – everyone's planning on this."

Everyone, apparently, except the one who would need to *live* it. So how did "everyone" get the idea that this young person was to become a veterinarian, you ask?

Was it a family tradition or legacy? Was her mother or father also a veterinarian? Was she to follow in the footsteps of a favorite family member or mentor? Well, no.

She was to become a veterinarian because twelve years earlier, while petting a kitten, she said she wanted to be a vet. Imagine that. Based on that criteria, I'm amazed that there are *any* other career choices for young women!

I asked the mother if it were possible that the family had built this dream around a false assumption. That at six years old, many children see being a veterinarian as a sort of fun way to spend a significant amount of time petting kittens and puppies, but not necessarily desiring to make a life out of spaying, neutering, or otherwise performing medical procedures on them.

More importantly, while the family was looking in a different direction, this girl had developed a ton of really outstanding dreams of her own, and a desire to make them real. My conversation with the daughter ended up shedding a ton of light on her passion. It was also fairly concise:

> Me: "Look out ten years, how do you envision your life?"
>
> Her: "I want to make some good money, buy a house – not have any debt at all."
>
> Me: "Well, veterinarians get paid pretty well. Do you want to have a family?"
>
> Her: "Definitely!"
>
> Me: "And what does your future family life look like?"
>
> Her: "I want to have kids and I definitely don't want to work full-time!"
>
> Me: "Why is that important to you?"
>
> Her: "I don't want my children in daycare – and I want to homeschool them!"
>
> Me: "How does becoming a veterinarian line up with the vision you have for yourself and your family?"
>
> Her: "It doesn't – at all!"

I suggested she follow her vision – and she has.

We all have decision points in our lives.

Right now, you are on the verge of writing and publishing your first book. Along with that comes the potential for tremendous rewards – the ability to call your own shots, the freedom to schedule your own days, the financial rewards of self-employment, the recognition of your peers, and the opportunity to leave a real mark on any piece of the world you choose.

What decisions have you made?

Chapter 2
Your Readers Are Waiting

"What great thing would you attempt
if you knew you could not fail?"
- Robert H. Schuller

W hat if I told you right now that I already had readers lined up for your new book? Sight unseen, credit cards in hand – ready to buy. And not just a few either.

Play along with me.

And now imagine also that the initial numbers are going to be somewhere between 12,000-18,000 softcovers on Amazon and Barnes & Noble, and another, oh... I don't know, maybe 60,000-80,000 downloads on Kindle and Nook.

Still with me?

To summarize:

1) You have a boatload of people eager and somewhat impatiently waiting to go online and purchase the book you have in your head.

2) This will result in a significantly sweet profit for you and forever put to rest the question of, "Are you still writing that *thing?"*

3) There is absolutely zero possibility of failure – your readers are committed to purchase whatever it is that you produce.

Sound good? Then I also have three questions:

1) What are the main challenges to your work being completed and published?

2) Would you like the secret to annihilating these obstacles with just one action?

3) How are you feeling this very second?

More than likely, the truth is that I already have a pretty good idea about your answer to the first question – that which asks what factors *you* are still allowing to hold you back. They are the same habits, issues, and influences that are stopping countless others from breaking out – keeping them from realizing their true potential, following their deepest and most protected dreams, and living a life that overflows with passion and purpose.

Fear, doubt, worry. Issues of self-worth or competence. Procrastination. Perfectionism. Unrealistic expectations, or excuses such as disorganization, or lack of time or money or connections.

Next, I also know the answer to question number two. Of course you want to learn the secret to eliminating these challenges, and I am going to give it to you. We are going to address each of these unproductive and negative influences, and in the process render them forever powerless to steal the peace, joy and success you deserve.

Finally, the answer to question three is more personal. Just how *do* you feel right now? You may be excited or hopeful about your path, sensing that this really is your time to shine.

You may be eager to get your project underway, produced, and marketed – to say what you want to say and to have your ideas accepted.

Or you may be guarded – possibly apprehensive – unwilling to show your emotions for fear of also being called a dreamer by people you respect and love.

Trust me, I know.

And it's on this third point that we will continue to check in. Yes, how are you feeling right now matters a great deal. What changes are you experiencing right now? What are you believing about yourself right now? How strong is your desire to improve yourself, your relationships, and your world – right now?

This is such an important concept, because the connection that you have with yourself will ultimately become the connection you have with your audience.

A moment ago, I asked about the strength of your *desire.* I love that word. And, in this book, beginning with the introduction and throughout the first chapter, we have spoken of that emotion – your desire. Your dreams, your passions, your yearning to reach your potential and touch others with your work, your life, your art. I encourage you to begin there – know your desire – and never stray too far.

As you evaluate your current circumstances and plan for your future, as you begin to work that plan – developing your thoughts, forming your words, and creating your stories – as you stand on your integrity and become a leader and person of influence, stay connected to your desire.

It contains the seeds of your inspiration.

My wife, Kathy, is truly inspiring. Having met as teenagers, she has also been a subject of my desire going all the way back to childhood. Yesterday, she and I were speaking about this book and how it is laid out. Looking at the Table of Contents and the various parts and chapter titles, it quickly became evident that our desire – our goal and passion and purpose – is to see you achieve *your* dream, to fulfill the calling of *your* heart, leave whatever legacy is important to *you*, and get *your* awesome work published.

And all of that begins with embracing *your desire.*

As mentioned a moment ago, you and I are about to remove the most common hangups and challenges from your work as an author and thought leader. Your commitment to a handful of overriding principles will eliminate them from your life forever, but you must desire to do so.

Take note that throughout this book, regardless of the subject matter, I will keep you close to your passion – your desire. Please hear this. Knowing *why* you desire to do anything is more important than knowing *how* you are going to do it.

The how will happen. You *will* figure it out. In the meantime, fan the flames of desire that reside in your heart – that burn away the fear, worry, and procrastination, as well as the past hurts, guilt, and failure.

"Desire for change or improvement always comes first," Kathy told me. "You can believe in yourself and others, but if you don't *really* desire to see a different outcome, you won't have the courage to face your fears, overcome the setbacks, and weather the storm of criticism that often comes."

How right she is!

Over many years, I have personally witnessed my wife's strength, courage, and passionate desire to see others thrive in an environment of acceptance and excellence.

This is absolutely a lesson she can teach as well as anyone I've ever met.

The Happiest Place On Earth

Walt Disney is famous for saying that, "All our dreams can come true, if we have the courage to pursue them."

Of course, some people will immediately jump on his words and exclaim that such a statement is easy to make when, well... you're Walt Disney!

But it wasn't always the case.

For much of his career, Walt Disney faced incredible opposition, from within and without his inner circle. In 1954, as he began work on 160 acres of orange groves and walnut trees in Anaheim, CA, Walt envisioned a place that would be as attractive to adults as it was to their children – a place where they could really enjoy spending time together.

He could see the future, the fun, the families. He sensed the desire that parents had, the desire for entertainment and education that would neither bore nor offend, an environment of safety away from the carnival atmosphere that dominated the "theme parks" of the day.

Disneyland would be a "small world in itself, encompassing the essence of all the things that were good and true in American life." It would "reflect the faith and challenge of the future... and offer intelligently presented facts, the stimulation of the imagination, the standards of health and achievement, and above all, a sense of strength, contentment, and well being."

Pretty cool vision – but not everyone saw it the same way. Banks denied him. Investors balked, acquaintances scoffed. Even friends laughed and ridiculed, refusing to join him in business. After all, he was *just a dreamer.*

Yes, Walt Disney was a dreamer! And his dream began with his passion and desire to create what he called "the happiest place on earth." This was a dream he had, first for his daughter, then for his family – and ultimately for your family and mine.

It is exactly what he created.

Now, please hear what I am about to say, because the same success is available for you right now. Disney lived in the *happiest place on earth* because he got up each day and moved the dial forward on achieving his dreams. The happiest place was in his own mind, just as you desire it to be for you.

The success isn't in the dollars – it's in the doing.

There is something very special about clearly defining your vision, setting out some plans, and going to work at once with whatever tools, team, and resources you have.

Right now, you have a vision to become an author – to have your works published.

Through that vision, people you have never met will be inspired and entertained, filled with hope or sentiment, educated and encouraged to take up new challenges and interests, or be transported to a place of *their own* dreams.

By getting up and pursuing your dreams, new ideas will be created and new relationships will form – along with new opportunities.

You began with a desire to write and are suddenly excited to learn that there has never been a better time in the history of the world to accomplish that goal. You are now being equipped with knowledge and belief in yourself – the conviction that there is no one more qualified to express your deepest passions than you are. With each page your confidence grows, knowing that help is available to walk you *step-by-step* through the publication and distribution process – to get your thoughts and words and stories out to the world. And as you travel this road, you begin to live in a very special and unique environment.

For there is no happier place on earth than wherever you happen to be *if* you are at peace with yourself. If you really know who you are, what's important, and why.

If you are authentic.

We spoke of this authenticity in the previous chapter and we'll return to it shortly to see how its positive application can eliminate most of the factors that may currently have you tied in knots, procrastinating instead of publishing – wishing instead of writing.

So what's stopping you? And how can you simply and effectively and permanently go over, around, and through the obstacles?

I'll Do It... Someday

Have you ever heard those words before? Have you ever used them? If so, have you ever asked yourself *why* you used them?

The truth is that, at this very minute, we are either doing what it is we want to do and living the life we want to live, or we're not. And if not, we either have a written and specific plan to change our actions and behavior, or we don't. And *if* we don't, it is quite likely that "someday" will never come. In fact, like "tomorrow," it never arrives. We have today, period. It's all we've ever had – and all we ever will.

Now, please understand, if this message is resonating with you, you are not alone. Like waves on the sea, I have experienced my share of ups and downs, success and failure, production and procrastination.

And here is what I've learned:

The up times, generally accompanied by success and production, are far preferable to the down times, which are often recognized by their bouts of failure and procrastination.

In fact, procrastination is typically nothing more than a symptom that other factors are at work. When we procrastinate, we are, by definition, putting off doing the things that need to be done to complete whatever activity, goal, or project that we have put on our list to accomplish.

In looking at my own patterns of procrastination, and in speaking and coaching hundreds of individuals over the years, the first sign that procrastination is at play can often be found in the excuses that we tell ourselves and others about why we haven't done something that we said we would do.

"As soon as I finish x or y or z... as soon as I feel better... as soon as we get through this health issue with so-and-so... then I'll get started."

"Right now, I just don't have the time."

"I don't have the money."

"I don't have the contacts."

"I don't have the plan."

"I need to do more research."

"I need to get my ducks in a row."

When we use these phrases and verbally justify why we aren't doing something – or why we can't do something – and we repeat them over and over again, we ultimately begin to believe our own excuses and rationalize our failure to act. It is one of the quickest paths to nowhere!

Now let me give you some good news.

Most of these excuses are just that – excuses – and after today they will no longer have the power to control you.

You are about to write and publish your first book. You can begin today. If you sincerely find yourself frazzled and at your wits' end about how to manage it all, I recommend that you visit http://NewMediaJet.com/inspire where you will receive a chart to assist you to organize your time, and several other terrific tools and ideas to get you started today.

Until then, let me say this about time, and then address the more common excuses given previously. You *have* the time that you have – it is all the time that there is. And now I'll take you back to the opening quote of this chapter, because for most of us, it is not a time issue at all:

"What great thing would you attempt
if you knew you could not fail?"

If you knew that the success or reward you are seeking was right in front of you, and you simply had to claim it – that you could not fail – would time really matter, or would you simply *make* the time and take the prize?

I believe that most often, the lack of time (or money, or connections, or plan for that matter) are not really issues at all. It is likely that more research or planning or organizing *are not* required to win. Consider for a moment that, at least for now, the ducks are as lined up as they're going to get.

And then ask yourself this: "Do the ducks really care?"

Suppose, for example, that you receive a call today from a friend who lives just shy of three hours away. She wants you to know that she has just won a brand new BMW, all taxes paid – and all expenses paid, including insurance, fuel, and maintenance for a year. It is to be delivered next Monday morning, promptly at ten o'clock.

What does this have to do with you?

Well, it just so happens that the car is too small for her family, won't fit in their garage, and while it would be a fun ride, they just have a ton of other priorities right now. Besides which, your friend knows your car has been giving you trouble, she knows you love the brand, and it just happens to be your favorite color. She also remembers the kindness that you showed when you helped her out a few years ago in a desperate situation.

What does she want for it? The special delivery charge is $300, payable at the appointed time and place. If you can be there and pay the fee, the car is yours.

The decision is up to you. Will you rearrange your schedule? Can you find the time? Is the money really a major setback? How much planning or organizing or research do you need to do? How many ducks need to be lined up, or does the priority of receiving this beautiful automobile – this work of art – temporarily override those other concerns?

I believe we both know the answer, and the same holds true for every other important goal, mission, or purpose that you have in your life. If the vision is big enough, these other factors are mere distractions – potential obstacles of procrastination to be gone over, around, or through. Likewise, you may find that the rewards associated with writing and publishing your work will easily overcome the excuses associated with procrastination.

Later in this chapter, I am going to show you that your market is already made and your readers are eager to buy. This truth, coupled with belief in both yourself and this system, can provide you with all the benefits you are seeking, such as the ability to:

1) Get your ideas and stories out to the world.
2) Share your values and insights with your children and grandchildren.
3) Be recognized by your friends, family, co-workers, and peers.
4) Attain the expert status you both desire and deserve.
5) Regain the freedom to work for yourself and on your own terms.
6) Raise awareness or increase resources for causes you champion.
7) Leave a lasting legacy in writing for future generations.

How do the excuses compare then?

No time? There is no time but the present. No money? You can publish your book for under $100. No contacts? There's no need to play those games ever again – schmoozing execs and editors with the big publishers. No plans? Don't worry, we've got help available online. More research? That's typically just a delay tactic – check your vision and begin with the assets and knowledge you have.

Lining up ducks? They're ducks... they'll wait.

Fear Not

Procrastination is common. It is widespread and affects all cultures, demographics, and professions. In some respect or another, we are all affected by procrastination – either of our own making or of someone else's.

The trouble is that procrastination can be extremely elusive, and the real reasons behind our delays and hesitations are often well-protected, hidden securely beneath the excuses, rationalizations, and justifications that seem to work so well in projecting the image we want to project.

As I studied and analyzed my own procrastination over the years, I ran headlong into a truth that I'd like to share now. In the past, the reason I tended to excuse and rationalize and justify – to blame lack of time or money or resources – was because it allowed me a believable distraction from the discomfort of facing feelings I didn't necessarily want to deal with.

In any of our lives, the list may be long and might include doubt, confusion, worry, inadequacy, rejection, or many others. And they all lead to one place – fear. Doubt reveals a fear that the decision will be unsuccessful. Confusion leads to fear that the wrong decision will be made. Worry reveals fear of the future. Inadequacy and rejection point to fears of one's unworthiness or inability to perform. Now this is important. Fear, as found in any of the examples above, is largely based on the unknown. It lives beyond the comfort zone – it is off the edge of the map.

Early explorers had to deal with such fears. Young sailors heading out to sea were confronted with a host of challenges – many of which were very real. Depending on the integrity of their ship – and the skills of their shipmates – they may or may not ever return to the land that they called home. They were leaving family and friends in search of treasure – fortune and fame. Their equipment and ability to navigate through intense storms, to carry enough food and pure drink, all played a significant role in their safety. This was a time in history when rats, spoiled provisions, or disease could eliminate the entire crew, turning a magnificent vessel into a solitary ghost ship.

And *then* there were the monsters.

While each expedition yielded new information and expanded the horizons, there was still the edge of the map – the edge of the known world. What lay beyond, no one could be sure. But if there *were* monsters, it was likely that this was where the sailors would meet them, for it was a place that allowed imaginations to run wild.

They had heard the stories. Read the stories. Believed the stories. And when doubt crept in, when weather conditions led to confusion, as worry and fear set upon them... they saw monsters. Monsters of their own making.

If we're not careful, the unknown has a way of creating such monsters in our own life:

"This is just a pipe-dream... who am I kidding?"

"I tried this before and got rejected, why will it work this time?"

"What if I write this book, and can't get it published?"

"What if I get it published, and no one buys it?"

"What if my friends and family don't like it?"

"Worse, what if they laugh at me?"

"What even qualifies me to write it?"

"So many people try and fail... what makes me think I'm any different?"

"How am I going to market it?"

"How am I going to sell it?"

"How do I even begin pulling my thoughts and ideas and writing together?"

"What if I lose money?"

"What if... there really *are* monsters out there?"

I want you to stand up, take a deep breath, and go get a pen and some paper to write on. Go ahead, do it now.

At the top-left, write the words, "Best Case."

At the top-right, write the words, "Worst Case."

Now draw a line down the center of the page, and then ask yourself this question: "If I pursue my vision, if I write and publish my book, my stories, my ideas, my poetry, my passion – what could happen?"

Yes, what are the *best possible outcomes* if all of your dreams come true and the book becomes a bestseller?

Think of the sense of accomplishment, the power you feel from facing and overcoming your fears. Soak for a moment in the admiration of your friends or family or co-workers, and relish the ability to add some extra-special touches to your own life or the life of someone you care for deeply. Experience the freedom to really travel again, homeschool or tutor-school your children, bless your parents or grandparents if they are still with us, or give to charity, give of your time, or give of your wisdom and knowledge. Imagine completing a plan to mentor our youth, pioneer a program, or learn a new language or two. You might adopt a child, sponsor a child, become a spokesperson for your favorite cause, or get involved in your community, church, or political organization of choice.

Create a bucket-list, take up a musical instrument or two, attend the World Series or Superbowl... what do you desire? Heck, you might just take a few of your new writing and publishing skills and start your own business, publishing for profit part-time from home for any of the countless thousands of budding authors who are looking for help getting their own works published! You can explore this possibility further at http://NewMediaJet.com/publish.

Go ahead and put your ideas and dreams on paper – any circumstances that fall within your best case scenario.

Now... you know what's coming. On the other side of your paper, write what could happen in the *worst case* if you follow your dream and you sell only three copies to your spouse or your friend or your mom.

Okay... give me a minute, I'm thinking.

Hang on – I said I'm thinking! What is the worst that could happen?

Well, I don't know – I suppose you may be out a few dollars, and...

And... I think that's it. A few bucks.

Of course, the safest bet – the place where you'd never travel to the unknown – is to do nothing. Put your passion on ice, your dream on hold, your fear in the driver's seat. But I believe you've come too far to ever allow that again.

No One Is Perfect

There are so many fabulous reasons to write – so many inspiring stories to tell – and just a few powerful emotions or traits that tend to keep our creativity and production all bottled up.

Here are two more: competence and perfectionism.

In a discussion with a family friend, she related that there were some very important and urgent activities that weren't getting done – activities that she really felt needed to be accomplished in order for her to stay on track.

We spoke for a few minutes, about fear and about priorities – all the textbook stuff. She said she didn't have any of those issues in her life, and then exclaimed, "I just have no idea why I am not getting these things done!"

Then I asked her about competence.

You see, she is one of the most competent people I have ever met, at least in all her areas of competence!

We looked at her list of *musts* and *have-to's* that had gone undone, and I asked her if it were possible that she was not doing these other things because she did not yet feel competent doing them.

Bingo! That is what you call nailing it!

This was pointed out to me some years back when I was struggling with the very same set of circumstances. I was extremely competent in *everything* I did, simply because I didn't do *anything* in which I wasn't competent.

Next, we went over her calendar, and found that her schedule was packed full of things at which she is very good... in fact, extremely good. But this left little time to devote to improving in the other areas that were critical to the achievement of her goals.

This can really become a stumbling block to learning, and to action. In fact, the need to be completely competent – to be perfect – can actually stop action altogether. And it is harder to start again the next time.

The advice I received all those years ago is still very valid: "The secret to becoming very good at something," I was told, "is to be willing to not be perfect at it for a while."

"Be willing to try and fail," I suggested. "What's the worst that could happen? And you might even succeed!"

Just three days later, I got the call. What call, you ask?

The call that said everything – yes, everything – had changed since our talk a few days earlier. Everything – as in new life plan, new health plan, new business plan. Oh yes, and she's going to write a book – in fact, a *series* of books.

And all this change came with a transformation in her

attitude and outlook. Of course, those emotions must now be sustained, but oh my – is she off to a great start!

This point deserves repeating. Competence and perfection can be opposite sides of the same coin, and either can really hang us up. When we feel the need to be highly competent at everything we do, we often limit the number of activities and dreams that we will pursue.

If this becomes the expectation – and ultimately our identity – we may begin to only attempt those things which we are *certain* to do with near perfection.

The problem is that most goals that are big enough to be worthy of our time, focus and energy cannot be accomplished without going through a fair amount of personal growth, a steep learning curve, or some serious testing of our mettle.

And "near perfection" doesn't live there – yet.

When we stick to the stuff that we're already good at, we sacrifice our ability to improve other skills that are critically important to the overall success of our idea or venture. Yes, we sacrifice our goal, our purpose – even our mission itself.

The moral and beauty of this story is that in just seventy-two hours, my friend faced one of her greatest challenges and accomplished a vitally important step – an integral piece of a much bigger goal – one that had been languishing undone for months.

More importantly, her decision to act, backed up by the willingness to do so, has since set off a powerful chain reaction of opportunities that would have otherwise passed unnoticed from the viewpoint that she had held just days earlier.

A New Perspective

I began this chapter with a simple question – and an even simpler idea. If the buyers were already lined up and the sales already made, would you be willing to accept some advice, schedule the time, and put your amazing ideas or stories into a document that could be easily published and delivered to them?

Further, if you knew that you didn't have to be pushy or convince or persuade – didn't have to face objection or rejection – would that make your life and decisions any easier? Yes, if you believed in your heart that your life could change and that you could begin living your dream today, would you do it?

Well, the good news is that your readers are not only assembled, ready, and waiting – they're actively searching!

In fact, in the time it has taken you to read this far, hundreds of thousands of people – perhaps millions of people – have searched both online and in quality booksellers across the nation for whatever information, entertainment, or inspiration that will fill the hole that they want filled. It matters little the subject of their desire – emotional, physical, spiritual, financial, or relational – what matters is that they're looking.

And as unique and individual as we sometimes feel and believe our desires to be, we nevertheless live in a world with billions of other people, with whom we share many values, ideas, qualities, and beliefs.

Importantly, as a writer – as a thought leader – *you* have something to add to the conversation, or you wouldn't be reading this book.

In the next chapter, we'll look at how technology

stands ready to connect you with your potential audience in what may become the biggest dance – and greatest joy – of your life.

But first, I promised that I would share the secret to eliminating all of the obstacles – the fear, procrastination, doubt, or self-image issues – that have kept you from completing your project once and for all.

Write From The Heart

I want to take the pressure off you now. From this point forward, I want you to write as if you're speaking with a good friend, a family member, or someone whom you care for deeply. Someone with whom you have life in common.

Someone you can show your heart.

Let's start just by acknowledging a few desires that we share and experience, as writers, as readers, and as people just making our way through life.

We all want to be loved.

We want to be accepted.

And not just that, most of us also want to be noticed, appreciated, respected, sought-after, and valued.

Yes, valued. We want to know that we bring something to the table – that we are making a difference and an impact. We want to know that our lives matter – that our ideas are valuable – that we can change and improve circumstances just by the way we think. And one of the ways we do that is to give of ourselves, to share our time and influence and ideas – by writing.

It doesn't matter what category, type, or genre you love, my advice is always the same – go with your heart. Whether your passion is nonfiction, poetry, fantasy, history, or mystery – it's all the same. From romance to religion, cookbooks to computers, or fitness to family – whatever your passion, go with your heart.

The reason I say this is simple – *that* book is already written. I tell you to go with your heart because you're never far from it. There is no need for pretense – no need for research. You feel, you write – and you connect.

However, the challenge is that some of us have spent years – even decades – performing daily to achieve a dream and a vision that wasn't really ours. We allowed that seventeen year old – and the expectations of others – to determine our life-path. We've gotten away from diligently pursuing those things that provide us the greatest joy – that we hold most dear.

This is a common cause of writer's block. We want to write from the heart, and from our passion, but if we stay away from our passion long enough – or if our belief in accomplishing our dream fades – we can reach a place where we're not really even sure what's so important anymore. It's important to know *what's* important – stay close to your heart.

I was speaking to a friend who confided that she hadn't written in months. It had been over two years since she had put together a basic outline for her book, and now found herself frustrated, wondering if she should even continue with that project or switch to a new title altogether.

Having recently imposed several hard-deadlines on herself, she was really struggling. I suggested she find an issue that was really important to her – something she truly valued.

Suddenly, it all came pouring out.

"That's just it, Steve," her voice trembled. "I honestly don't even know what's important anymore."

Knowing that we tend to spend our resources, and particularly our money and our time, on things that we value, I asked if we could do a small exercise. I suggested she concentrate diligently on the following scenario for three hours, and then call me back with a plan.

"Suppose I gave you one hundred thousand dollars, with three stipulations," I began. "First, you can't buy anything for yourself. Second, you can't use it to pay debt. And third, you must give it all away within twenty-four hours."

Without hesitation, she stated that she didn't need three hours. She was excited, energized – passionate!

"There are two women's shelters in this county, and I would give each one thirty thousand. Next, I would give twenty grand to this legal advocacy service over here that helps women who are victims of domestic violence. And finally, I can think of two broken families from my church who I'd give ten thousand apiece just to send them away on a vacation or something." Done – with time to spare!

I doubt if it was any more difficult for you than it was for me to catch a common thread of passion in that conversation – an insight into her world about what is ultimately and truly important to her. Today, she is back in school, as an adult student at an online university, getting a degree in domestic counseling. She has put together plans to organize a women's retreat and safe-house.

And once again, she's writing.

Now, I've heard it all before, so I know that right now, someone – possibly even you – is thinking, "Well, sure, I can see that your friend's passion includes healing problems that exist in a large percentage of the homes in the country. That's life-changing. In fact, that's life-saving! But my passion, well... it isn't that heavy. You see, I'm *just* a..."

Stop. If you take nothing else away from this book, take this: your passion is your passion and you are important. It doesn't matter what you're into – out of the hundreds of millions of Americans and the billions of others around the globe, there are, at minimum, many thousands of people who are just as passionate as you are about whatever it is you're passionate about, *and* who will be both blessed and honored to buy a copy of your awesome new book. They may even ask you to sign it!

And they also have a network of friends, acquaintances, and associates who are likely into many of the same doggone things. Isn't that amazing? In fact, I wouldn't be surprised if it was the common interest that you all share that helped solidify the friendship in the first place. And more exciting is the truth that every person in the network, has a network!

In Chapter 4, I'll give you an exercise to help you zone in on those things that matter most to you, and at http://NewMediaJet.com/inspire, I'll also share my own.

Identify your passion, live your passion, write your passion. When you do, you'll attract readers who believe and feel and study and enjoy the same subjects and activities, and that eliminates the fear that comes from being way out in the unknown. There is no fear between friends. No apologies are necessary when living your values.

When you lead with your heart, you lead with yourself – and your readers get to know your thoughts, words, ideas, humor, wisdom, values, insights, experience, and advice. So, c'mon... let's not keep them waiting.

Chapter 3

Technology Makes It Easy

"The future belongs to those who believe
in the beauty of their dreams."
- Eleanor Roosevelt

This week I began working with friends on a terrific project that will be absolutely transformational to the lives of a select group of individuals who have had about enough.

Enough waiting, enough stress, enough procrastination. Enough average and mediocre and ordinary. Enough settling for second-best.

Enough of others' expectations, enough conformity and limitations. Enough unfulfilled potential, enough putting off dreams. Enough living in the future – enough living in the past.

Enough of the same work with the same results and the same rewards. Enough despair, frustration, and drama. Enough judgment and ridicule. Enough fronts and faking and one-ups and game-playing. Enough fear and guilt and shame and pain and silence and loneliness. Enough hopelessness and blame.

Enough.

And so I'm wondering… is it possible that you, too, have had enough? The reason I ask is simple. As we've invested the last hour or so together – as we carefully read the introduction and the opening chapters – several truths have become abundantly and undeniably clear:

1) You are absolutely and distinctly qualified to write and publish all of your current and future work.

2) Your market – your readers – are ready, willing, and waiting to buy.

Now read those two truths again – go ahead – and then don't be surprised if you suddenly feel some significant anticipation and joy, some real excitement in your spirit, as you discover truth number three:

3) Never in the history of the world has so much power, so much capacity, and so much technology been lined up and made available at so small a cost, just to make all your hopes and dreams come true.

Technology – Simple Tools That You Can Use

Many years ago, while visiting my dad at his office, his secretary asked if I had a minute to help her, and then went on to express frustration over the new "word processor" she was working with. It seemed her old typewriter was *so* much easier to use and this new "thing" on her desk just wasn't working right.

It is important to note that she also believed carbon paper (for those who remember it) was so much easier as well!

In any event, I clarified a few of the basic commands – yes, commands – and we found out her new machine was working just the way it was designed, primitive as it was by today's standards.

Shortly thereafter, I suggested to my dad that if he learned to use that "thing," we could easily save all of his files digitally and who knows what we might do with it all *someday*. You see, he was in his early sixties at the time, many of his friends were beginning to retire and grow old quickly, and I was intent upon helping him to create a brand new 20-year plan to stay in the game.

Now, there are three other insights you should know:

1) This was at a time in history where an extraordinary percentage of the population over college age was afraid to turn on a computer for fear that "it might blow up."

2) I have always believed that retirement without a clear purpose or plan is a fast track to premature aging.

3) My parents have always been incredibly active and engaged – a truth which has been a continual source of joy for me throughout my life.

In fact, I would imagine that this third point has had much to do with my own visions and missions and purposes, one of which is helping others to *do their best* – and to *be their best* – by helping them to *feel their best* through nutrition and exercise.

Please allow me to share this personal side of my life with you, and then I'll tie it all together with the technology message of this chapter. As I just intimated, anyone who knows me well is familiar with my incredible passion for nutrition, health, and wellness – for myself and for others. If, on the other hand, you and I are only just now getting to know one another, then let me state this very clearly: I am absolutely passionate about nutrition, health, and wellness!

The source of my passion is simple.

Throughout my formative years, from grade school right through college, I was always incredibly active and in fairly decent shape.

However, in my mid-twenties, I started a business and along with it came long hours, lack of exercise, an increasing number of unhealthy meals, additional stress, and – believe it or not – unwanted pounds.

Over the next 23 years, I bought into every reputable diet and workout program I could find as I struggled to lose the extra 35-50 pounds that I consistently carried... and none of them were effective long-term.

I was frustrated and felt out-of-control because nothing that I tried seemed to be even remotely sustainable in achieving the goals I had set.

Yet, here's what's important.

Through it all, I never lost sight of my dream to be wildly healthy again. I wanted to remove the ball and chain that I carried with all that extra weight. I wanted to wake up and have an abundance of energy to go and enjoy whatever came each day – to have stamina and mental focus and clarity.

And I wanted to fit into trim clothes again!

So what does all this have to do with you – with your writing, or with technology?

Well, actually everything.

It was technology and the Internet that allowed me to connect with new friends who selflessly introduced me to the science and healthy principles that changed my life.

It was technology and the Internet that made possible three years of research on the best products and programs available in the country.

It was technology and the Internet that provided a network of trainers and coaches at no cost to help me achieve my goals.

It was technology and the Internet that gave me a portal to the writings, journals, newsletters, books, blogs, videos, documentaries, and websites of health professionals.

It was technology and the Internet that granted me the ability to study for certifications in sports nutrition and personal training.

It was technology and the Internet that published and put this book into your hands right now, and it is technology and the Internet that will publish and put your awesome works into the hands of your reader.

Most importantly, it is technology and the Internet that has made this opportunity available to virtually everyone, and at a price that fits into every budget.

Every single one.

Which brings me back to my story.

The majority of my exercise comes on the seat of my bicycle, riding through the countryside 24-30 miles at a time, usually lost in my thoughts and ideas about the next book or article I'm writing or what I have to accomplish for one of the many irons that I have in the fire.

However, on occasion in the evening, instead of cycling, I find myself out walking, just for a change in routine.

Not running – not jogging.

Walking.

Now, if you've recently been stepping out and walking in your neighborhood after dark, you have no doubt become aware that, while you are getting your exercise, there are a lot of your neighbors who *are not* out walking after dark. No, if your neighborhood is anything like most of the other neighborhoods in the country, your neighbors, rather than exercising, are mostly gathered around a pale blue flickering light in their living rooms.

So it was the other night that as I approached a "T" in the road, I couldn't help but observe an elderly woman sitting right in front of a large picture window. The drapes were wide open and, yes, the faint blue flickering light was there also.

But here's the really cool part.

As I got closer, two things became very clear. First, this woman was *much* older than I had first realized, and second, this light she was staring at was from her laptop – not her television set. In fact, as near as I could tell, her TV wasn't on at all – instead of just staring, she was surfing! She was active! She was alive!

And as I was headed home to continue working on this book for you – a book that will show you the way and offer you resources to use today's amazing technology to write and publish your book – I just felt really good about that.

It is so different than the mindset of a few decades ago, when an entire generation tuned out of the advances that could have brought them happiness and kept them in a mode of personal growth.

It brings me joy to know that people, especially those in my parents' generation and older, are using the tools – and learning the technology.

I guess it's the same way I felt about my friend when she decided to go back to school after thirty-two years – this time *online.*

It's the sense of pride I get when I catch my dad – now past his mid-eighties – working on the computer at his desk and editing his own documents and manuscripts for the books that he is now excited about writing and publishing!

It's finding my mom playing with her mp3 or her new phone or wireless device, streaming video chats with her grandchildren, and talking about the stories she might like to tell. And it's producing resources like this book or our publishing course to help new friends like you to take your dreams and your life to the next level, to finally produce and publish your work for the benefit of yourself, your family, and others.

Technology – The Highway To Your Dreams

When I talk with people about writing and publishing, and especially about the technology side of writing and publishing, certain common threads and questions tend to run through the conversation.

Common, as in... they take place in about 90% of the interactions. It happened again last night.

After a fourteen-hour day that included multiple meetings on product creation, sales and marketing, online distribution and delivery of our books and training courses, and hours and hours sitting in my most comfortable chair with earplugs in my ears and my keyboard in my lap, I took a 40 minute break from my writing.

And as I often do on such breaks, I got in my car, set the cruise control, and cleared my mind as I drove the circuit of highways that form a sort of rectangular bypass of the city.

Brilliant moon. Cool, crisp air. Perfect evening.

Along the way, I stopped to fill my tank and pick up a large bottle of water for the ride. As I greeted the clerk, she exclaimed, "Well, you sure have a lot of energy for this time of the night!"

"Thanks," I said, "but I'm just on a break. I'll be writing and editing for at least a few hours yet tonight!"

"Really, what kind of writing do you do?"

And the conversation was off to the races.

"Any tips for someone who wants to write a book?"

"How do you get your stuff published?"

"How do you learn to do that?"

"How do you get on Amazon?"

"What about Kindle?"

"How do you connect with potential readers?"

"Isn't that all *really* complicated?"

"Can I buy your book and course?"

Imagine that. She has a book to write, a desire to get her story out, and all the very same questions everyone else has. Now, here is what I love. Just a few short years ago, that conversation would likely have sounded something like this:

"Any tips for someone who wants to write a book?" Answer: *just keep pluggin' away.*

"How do you get your stuff published?" *Really tough.*

"How do you learn to do that?" *Lots of hard knocks.*

"How do you get on Amazon?" *What's Amazon?*

"What about Kindle?" *Excuse me? What's Kindle?*

"How do you connect with potential readers?" *You'll need a six-figure marketing budget.*

"Isn't that all *really* complicated?" *Yes, it is.*

"Can I buy your book and course?" *Well, you could... if I could ever get it published...*

What a difference today! Now read once again – here, almost verbatim, is how our discussion *really* went:

"Any tips for someone who wants to write a book?"
Absolutely.

"How do you get your stuff published?"
That's the great part, technology makes it easy.

"How do you learn to do that?"
Technology makes it easy.

"How do you get on Amazon?"
Technology makes it easy.

"What about Kindle?"
Technology makes it easy.

"How do you connect with potential readers?"
Technology makes it easy.

"Isn't that all *really* complicated?"
Nope, technology makes it easy.

"Can I buy your book and course?"
Yes, technology makes it easy.

What a fabulous time to be a writer!

It's interesting, but very often when discussing the new technologies that really do "make it easy," the person with whom I'm speaking is often surprised to learn how many tools are available to them in their quest to see their books get written and published.

At times, though, it goes further than that.

They are shocked – actually offended – even angered to realize that they didn't know how simple it could be to change the direction of their work, their creation, their art – their life.

They seem to be asking, "How could I *not know* this?"

My answer is always the same. You know what you

know, when you know. You can't change that. You're here *now,* and you're learning *now.* Your time is *now.*

Now is the time, and you are the reason this book is being written. Now is the time, and you are the reason our publishing course was produced. They are for you – for now. You know, now. So you can do something, now.

And *now* is a good time for two reasons:

1) "Now" is the only time that we have in which to create our work and hone our craft and live our passion.

2) Right now, there has been an absolute convergence of the advance of technology, and the availability of that technology – to you!

Amazing new technologies are forever being created, and they are always available. However, that doesn't mean that they are always available to *you.*

The development and distribution of new technologies follow a specific curve, and are typically marked by one major obstacle to the general public upon introduction – the new products or services are often extremely expensive! They are also often classified as luxuries, or worse – fads.

A small percentage of people, known as *early adopters*, may pay the price. And if the technology is to survive, innovation develops rapidly, putting previous versions, models and iterations in the hands of increasingly greater numbers of consumers at a lower and lower cost. This is nothing new.

While researching another project a while back, I came across the following mainstream article from 1901. The story was certainly cause for talk, blaring in all capital letters the shocking headline that, "FARMERS USE AUTOMOBILES." Here it is for your reading pleasure:

FARMERS USE AUTOMOBILES.

Factories Kept Busy on Orders from
Country Chauffeurs.
Special to The New York Times

CHICAGO, Ill., March 1. – Farmers in the country adjacent to Chicago are taking up the automobile fad. Orders received from rustic purchasers indicate that the country roads in Illinois and Wisconsin this Summer will be filled with horseless vehicles. Summer resorts are stimulating the business, and, while the automobile trade in the cities has diminished, country orders are keeping the factories busy. Gasoline motor power automobiles are said to be the most in demand among farmers.

As I read this, I thought, "Great, just what we need – another fad. Farmers driving around in cars..." After all, anyone could have told you that cars would *never* catch on with the general public!

But before we smile or shake our heads about the thinking or lack of vision of people in our past, we should be quick to remember that this is a familiar pattern that repeats throughout history and even through our own lives.

Similar conversations were had around such common inventions and innovations as FM radio, refrigeration, jet propulsion and air travel, color television, personal computers, cellular technology, satellite radio, the Internet, social networking, flat screens, streaming video, and online media.

Yup, all just fads. That is, until they became "must-have's" that transformed our very lives and work and culture. Until they made fortunes for their inventors, and gave powerful tools to the rest of us who are looking to make our own mark in the world.

When opening my first small business in the mid-1980's, I decided to replace one "fad" product with another. After much thought, research and budgeting, I was about to get rid of my "electric" typewriter and buy my first brand-new desktop computer. I had heard that this little gem could give me the ability to do some basic spreadsheets and "form" letters, and eliminate forever the need for future purchases of *White-Out.*

The possibilities seemed endless!

It was a thing of beauty; dual floppies, a two-color monitor – orange characters on a black screen – and *absolutely no* hard drive. Now, please understand, it wasn't that it was so technologically advanced that it didn't *need* a hard drive... it was just so technologically challenged that it didn't have one!

Backing it up was a three-and-a-half-hour process every Friday late-afternoon-into-early-evening on sixty-seven floppy disks. As weird as that seems today, after an initial learning curve, it did make my life easier and justified the nearly two thousand dollars that I invested.

Then, less than a year later, it happened again.

I met Tom and his wife, Chris, the owners of a local computer firm, who unveiled yet another fad that I fell in love with: the Kaypro PC/286i.

Brand new out-of-the-box with an all-new, extra special "RGB" (Red, Green, Blue) monitor, basic maintenance plan, and a "modest" delivery and set-up fee, this beauty set me back a cool $5400. Quite a chunk for a relatively new business that was still considerably in debt, but Tom said it would do everything that I needed it to do – and more.

And here's the truly unbelievable part. It had – are you sitting down – a 30 MB hard drive!

"OMG!" I said. "How *big* is that?!"

You know what's coming, but I'll tell you anyway because it is absolutely true. Tom's response was, "Well, Steve, let's put it this way… you'll never need another computer!"

Now, I'll admit that little Kaypro *did* do everything I needed at the time – it took a load off my shoulders every day, for which I am still thankful when I think of it.

And though he was off just slightly with the "never need another computer" remark, the technology was certainly not a fad. In fact, its progression has led to the new and emerging tools and technologies that you will use today to accomplish your goal and vision and become a published author.

As I think back on that story, one of the most interesting components – to me, anyway – is the cost or investment factor, because it is the price of the technology that either eliminates or allows people to participate in the technology.

When I bought that first computer, literally none of my employees had one. Nor did any of my family members, friends or neighbors. The price tag simply took it off the table for most people, and the perceived benefits of making such an investment were too few. How radically that has changed! The same could be said for most of the technological advances we now enjoy every day, with many products having become so inexpensive – my last three mobile phones have been free – that they are practically disposable.

Most importantly for our discussion, though, is that the tools and technologies that make it easy to write, easy to publish, and easy to connect with your interests and your reader and your market, are now abundantly available and accessible to you.

Technology – Making Writing Easy

All the technology in the world wouldn't be worth a hill of beans if it made our job more confusing, time-consuming, and cumbersome. After all, writing isn't the only thing that most of us are doing!

On the contrary, we may be raising children or grandchildren, taking care of aging parents, balancing homes and careers and juggling a boatload of other priorities and expectations – others' and our own.

We may be running businesses, running for political office, or literally running just to stay healthy and active and energetic enough to keep up with it all. Between work on the job, chores in the home, and volunteer responsibilities in our communities, few of us are looking for ways to make our life or our leisure more difficult or costly.

We want technology to improve our life. To make it better. To make it faster and less expensive – to make it easy.

As writers, we have been given so many gifts. Just a few years ago, the process that you're about to engage in certainly wouldn't have been described as easy, and it absolutely *was not* inexpensive!

In fact, so much has changed and we take so much for granted – particularly because of the Internet – that it almost seems ridiculous to mention. Yet, it is on the foundation of the web – and particularly the introduction of nearly-universal high-speed web – that many of these other blessings are established.

I won't spend much time speaking about the pre-PC or pre-Mac world, the pre-Internet era, or the pain of dial-up, other than to ask you to imagine outlining, organizing, researching, writing, and assembling your book without the technology that you have at your fingertips today.

Think, for example, of conducting just a rudimentary research project, composed of basic fact-finding to back up your conclusions or add color to your story, and digging into demographic or geographic details to add depth and character and realism to your scenes, without the aid of the Internet.

Yes, take away the web, and something as simple as cataloging and providing citations in a bibliography – or creating proper footnotes or endnotes to keep you out of a copyright infringement lawsuit – becomes real work. Think of the past seven days and then ask yourself how much spare time you have to go spend hours manually searching records at the library.

Google is the most-used website in the world for one reason – people are looking for things. They are saying, "Help me find *x*." They are researching – just like you and I. And as a society, we have become accustomed to searching for what we want and getting it now. Finding something when and where we need it saves time and frustration and adds quality to our work and our lives at levels that cannot even be measured. And when web technology went mobile, it revealed an entire new layer of benefits and convenience to anyone with an equipped smart-phone or mobile device – at a cost, in many cases, of less than a dollar a day.

Suddenly, the research, the organization, the composing can be done anywhere. In fact, portions of this book have been written on the keypad of my mobile, while waiting in the car to pick up my wife or daughter, another family member, or a friend. How cool is that – all with free apps, free software, and other Open Source programs that you can download to do, well... just about anything.

In just a minute, I'd like to touch on just a few of the countless benefits that we, as writers, have available because of the culture and philosophy that includes Open Source... but first, something *really interesting* just happened that I'd like to share with you.

You wouldn't know this from looking at the page, but I just had a ten minute interruption between the previous paragraph and the one right before it.

Here we were, discussing technology and the web and how that technology has evolved to mobile devices, and suddenly my computer just totally froze – something it does occasionally, and possibly something that you've experienced a time or two in your life as well.

Typically, it is not an issue for three reasons:
1) I tend to save my work really often.
2) My document program auto-saves really often.
3) My document program has a decent recovery function if the computer locks up, there's a crash, or I have to do a forced restart.

However, as soon as the screen froze, I realized that I didn't remember saving for the last few minutes and couldn't be sure when the program's last auto-save had taken place.

So, for safety's sake, I simply reached for my mobile, took a picture of the screen, and then shut the computer down without worry. As it turned out, I had to retype two and a half paragraphs. But because of technology, one way or another, my words and my work are safe.

In addition to the free Open Source program I am writing with, I also have a bridge program that copies my document files to another hard drive every few minutes and an online backup that runs every time a file is changed. The bridge program is also absolutely free, and the backup program costs less than five bucks a month for complete peace of mind. In the event of a complete loss, I could access my work from any other computer and be back up and running in minutes.

Most important, though, is not just that the technology is available – but that it is available to you.

Now back to the concept of Open Source, because it has had a profound influence on the creation and innovation of tools and technology that you will use to turn your dreams of becoming a published author into a reality in the next 30-60 days or so.

Heck, if your book is pretty-well written and edited already, we can have you published and available on Amazon in softcover and Kindle versions quicker than that!

Now, whether or not you are familiar with the words "Open Source" matters little – it is the idea behind them that I want you to grasp.

Strict constructionists may argue that the term should only refer to software that was created in a collaborative environment, with the source code published and available for any qualified programmer to edit. For example, to help make my writing and research a snap, I use four Open Source technologies on a near-daily basis:

1) Mozilla's Firefox browser.

2) Android's Operating System.

3) WordPress blogging software.

4) OpenOffice – a powerful alternative to Microsoft Office, without the price tag.

Each of these are cutting-edge, all continually being improved and upgraded, all with community support and involvement – and all free. Free is good.

We've been talking here about how technology has made the writing of your book easy. In the remaining sections of this chapter, we will discuss how technological advances have made publishing easy – and how it has made connecting with your market easy. In each of these sections, I take a much broader view of the culture and philosophy that I believe began with the Open Source movement, and continues to evolve in the areas of free software, mobile apps, and crowd-sourcing.

Regardless of the definition, the point is that the tools for outlining, researching, creating, composing, formatting, and editing your book are available at a cost and investment that is fast approaching zero.

I'll touch again on the practical aspects of Open Source in Part 2, when we'll discuss the benefits of a tremendous blogging platform like WordPress in both the creation phase (Chapter 4) and the connection phase (Chapter 5).

In my opinion, WordPress is the epitome of the benefits of Open Source, and should be considered as both a creative and marketing tool.

I'd like to end this section by simply mentioning four additional technology tools that myself and others have found to make the writing experience easier and more enjoyable:

1) MP3 technology, which allows you to capture every thought and never miss a beat. These small, inexpensive, and easy-to-use recorders can be carried with you throughout the day, ready for the moment your inspiration strikes.

2) The "cloud," which offers you *unlimited* storage capacity for literal pennies. The ability to access and use software, or to backup or store your own files in a secure off-site location provides significant cost and time savings.

3) Talk-to-type speech recognition programs – the ultimate tool for the non-typist. This technology has come a long way since I bought my first (and what I thought at the time would be my last) program. Today's software actually works.

4) Read-back software, which allows you to edit your book by listening to it. I always proofread my work out loud so that I really hear what is written, yet even then it is possible, as the author, to look past mistakes without catching them. Listening to a third party (even a computer-generated, digital third party) read your manuscript back to you can often illuminate areas that need correction or clarity, and it allows others to listen in and offer suggestions as well.

I believe that the great authors of the past would have likely parted with a small fortune to possess the terrific tools that we can access today for little or next to nothing. If you are interested in products such as these, you may learn more at http://NewMediaJet.com/inspire.

Technology – Making Publishing And Distribution Easy

I want you to think about what you or a family member or friend currently do for a living. Or, just for the fun of it, pick any industry at random. Now, ask yourself these questions:

Over the past decade or so, how has technology impacted the day-to-day operations or the lines of communication? What about the engineering or production or sales processes? How has technology automated our offices? How many ideas and assumptions have been reworked? How many machines and how much equipment has been rendered obsolete? How much easier is it to get things done, and to get the product or service from Point A to Point B?

Regardless of the industry, from manufacturing to medical, insurance to retail, agriculture to education to utilities or banking or travel, advances in technology revolutionize the way we work – and the way we live.

And the publishing industry is no different.

There are four major game-changers that have stood the publishing world on its head and created unprecedented opportunity for you. In fact, taken together, they are about to make a profound and positive impact on your life, and technology breakthroughs are at the heart of each:

1) The ability to professionally self-publish your own work.

2) The availability of economical print-on-demand services.

3) Increasing desire for digital format and wireless delivery.

4) Long tail online business models (such as Amazon) that facilitate points one through three, contain unlimited shelf space, and significantly level the playing field for aspiring authors. This fourth point is powerful and will not only be discussed here in its relation to independent (indie) publishing and print-on-demand, but also in our next section on technology and connecting.

Right now, however, let's look more in-depth at each of these four amazing components. Growing up, more than once I heard the phrase, "If you want it done right, you've got to do it yourself," and I suppose there must be at least a grain of truth for sayings like this to weave their way into the fabric of our culture. However, *the more* I learned about business – about effective organizations, exceptional training, and powerful teamwork – *the less* I agreed with this statement.

As specialization became more deeply ingrained in our educational and economic systems, I believed that the answer was to find experts in whatever field you needed to get your project done – then hire them, clarify the expectations, and delegate the work and the outcomes.

It's a system that works well when you have the power to make such plans and decisions, or if you actually own the means of production and distribution.

Conversely, it's a whole different story when a handful of major players control the field tightly, and you must receive their permission to play.

In the early 1990's, that is exactly where tens or even hundreds of thousands of authors found themselves, boxed in on one end by the titans of the industry, and on the other end by second and third tier publishers, often known collectively as vanity press or vanity publishers, who would take every dime you had – then ask for a few more.

There were limited resources available and technology or training was scarce for someone who was looking to go it alone. If you were interested in self-publishing, two things were certain: the process was sure to be *very* time-consuming and *really* expensive.

At the time, I wanted to publish, however I was immersed in growing a new business. I had few liquid assets. I had no solution and none was on the immediate horizon. I wonder if you know anyone who has ever experienced similar feelings – I wonder about you.

Fast forward. What a difference a few years make!

Today, the availability of powerful low-cost and no-cost applications combined with the technical and logistical resources of the world's biggest distributors not only allows you to *professionally* publish and market your own work – to literally do it yourself – it also allows you to publish for others, potentially creating significant multiple revenue streams from the comfort of your own home.

I will give you additional food for thought on this opportunity, and other potential financial rewards, in Chapter 7. It is also covered in detail in our step-by-step video publishing course, where you'll receive everything you need to be up and running within 30 days or less.

The second key component of this revolution is the development and near perfection of *digital* print-on-demand services. In the past, the printing process required long set-up times and the creation of permanent printing plates. These added significant expense, the cost of which could only be offset by printing tens of thousands of copies, or more.

I remember a marketing job that I had produced for one of my companies many years ago. The director of the ad agency that was responsible for the work gave me a quote of nearly $15,000 for a thousand pieces. He smiled as he said the first one cost $14,000 – the remaining nine-hundred ninety-nine were only $1 apiece.

The digital printing process eliminates all that and allows your book to be printed and assembled from files that you edit and upload yourself. In a nutshell, print-on-demand literally means just that. Your books will be printed when they are demanded – in other words, when they are ordered, one at a time. They can also be printed and shipped from a provider near your customer to reduce delivery time. Simple and convenient – without waste or inventory – all at a relative cost of next-to-nothing.

My brother called me recently to say he had just been on Amazon to order a book I had co-authored. Seeing that it could be physically delivered in as little as two days, he asked about inventory.

There is none.

"If you were to order that book right now," I told him, "the order and the associated files would be forwarded to a premier regional printer close to your home, uploaded into the queue and printed in the next hour or so, and then assembled, bound, and covered within minutes after that."

As soon as the glue dries and the product passes quality control, it is packaged, labeled and ready for parcel pickup. The customer is billed, the printer and Amazon get their cut, and I walk away with a decent royalty while incurring *zero* up-front, out-of-pocket expense!

It all seems like a simple and perfectly natural process today, but it wasn't always that way. Several years ago, I walked into a convenience store near my house. In the entryway was a small table stacked high with paperback books about one of my favorite subjects – aviation.

Behind the table stood a man in his early eighties, a pilot who also happened to be the co-author. He had self-published the book in 1991 – about the same time I received my own private pilot certification – and had several tens of thousands of copies printed. For the past few decades, his job was to sign them and sell them wherever he could.

He was genuine, and easily connected with customers. I learned that he had spent most of his career as a salesperson, and he was good. He also used his age in the sales process to perfection. I suspect he sold many books that day, and plenty since. Of course I bought a copy. Two, in fact – one for my dad and one for me.

Until recently, for many authors, that was the process. Write your book, pay through the nose, order a truckload of your own books – roll the dice.

A third and monumental event occurred during the Christmas season of 2011, and marked a turning point for the publishing world in general, and for you as an author in particular. For the first time in many years, the number one gift wasn't clothes, jewelry, mobile phones, or video games. Instead, the most-purchased, most-given, and most-received product in the U.S. was the Amazon Kindle Fire. Depending on when you may be reading this, you could either be thinking, "Yes, I have one of those," or, "Wow, I remember those."

In any event, it was a watershed moment for the industry and showcased the desire that people have for interesting and inexpensive content, delivered over the airwaves to the device of their choice – right now, with no waiting.

And following a similar path, your reader doesn't even need to spend a bunch of money to participate. There are countless eBooks available for a few bucks (or less), and they read just fine on a free app available for your mobile.

Pretty sweet. And from an author's point of view, you could really hit the jackpot. eBooks that are written and formatted well, can sell really well. For your viewing and revenue enhancement pleasure, *Making Money With Kindle* is included with our online print publishing course at http://NewMediaJet.com/publish, and is also available separately as an easy, step-by-step course if you are interested in selling *only* in digital format.

Either way, once you learn the process, you can upload unlimited content for free, change and edit it easily, and have your book available for sale online at Amazon in as little as 24 hours. And the royalties – as high as 70% – are tremendous!

Finally, let's look at the concept or business model that made this whole opportunity possible. It is undergirded by the Internet and technology, and here's how it looks.

Say you walk into a traditional brick-and-mortar business... in our case, a local bookstore. What do you see?

Now, don't be sarcastic – I know you see books, so let me rephrase and ask the question in a slightly different way. What *don't* you see? The answer might surprise you.

What you *don't* see, is almost every book that has ever been written! In fact, even in a large national chain or franchise bookseller, as a percentage of what has been written and published throughout the centuries, there are hardly any books there at all!

There are a number of reasons for that, some of which you may agree with and others you don't. For example, some may be purely political in nature, with executive decisions being made to promote or discourage certain points of view.

Similarly, business considerations and relationships also play a part, with certain publishers currying favor over others. Every now and again, announcements are made to the effect that certain titles from certain publishers will simply not be carried due to competitive factors.

And then, of course, there is the fact that every retail environment only has so much shelf space. It is finite. The store simply wants to go with titles that have a proven track record, some significant dollars backing the marketing effort, and a large potential audience. Some niches are simply deemed too risky.

Enter Amazon.com, the online shopping cart, and the technology that created unlimited shelf space. Interestingly, the first time I ever heard the name Amazon, it was being described as the latest *fad* to hit the Internet, which was itself still being debated as a fad.

Of course, as we know now, Amazon is one of the top-ranked sites in the world; according to Alexa, one out of every eighteen people online yesterday visited the site.

That's one powerful fad. This business model, described by Chris Anderson in his blockbuster book, *The Long Tail: Why the Future of Business Is Selling Less of More*, creates a major contrast with traditional retailers – and an amazing opportunity for you.

Example Of Long Tail Distribution

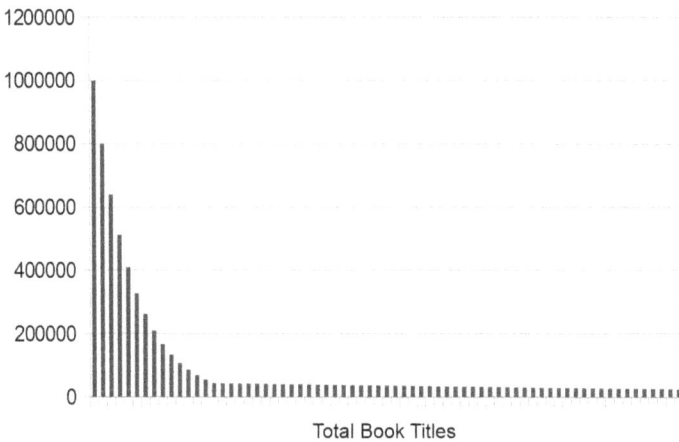

Total Book Titles

The name, Long Tail, derives from viewing the graphical distribution (see chart above) wherein a relatively few items sell massive numbers – *The New York Times Best Sellers* list, for example. You see that on the left side of the graph the numbers are very high.

These are the titles your local bookseller wants to carry... the ones that move. Now follow the curve down to the right, and notice the decreasing quantity of sales for additional titles – some may sell only a few copies a week, a month, or a year. These are the titles that local booksellers can't afford to carry.

But the list goes on forever! Millions and millions and

millions of titles! Your books and mine – the long tail. In fact, taken collectively, they represent far bigger sales numbers than all the bestsellers put together.

Amazon and similar sellers have no space problems, and they aren't concerned whether a book only sells 50 copies, or 50,000. The shelf space is available to us all – and, most importantly, to you – as long as you understand the process.

That is the source of my passion for writing this book – to clarify your vision and to encourage you to act. It is also the source of my passion in creating a comprehensive course on the process of independent publishing (also known as self-publishing or indie publishing) – to guide you *step-by-step* through publishing and distributing your first book within 30 days, and to publish anything you want, any time you want, for the rest of your life.

Technology – Making Connecting Easy

A number of years ago, Jeffrey Gitomer wrote that, "All things being equal, people want to do business with their friends. And all things being *not* so equal, people *still* want to do business with their friends."

Allow me to illustrate. Let's say the car is packed, the phone is charged, and the GPS is programmed. One last quick check of the house, and you're ready to go.

Oh yes, just one other thing – you must stop for gas before hitting the highway. You have two choices: immediately to your right is a Shell station, and at the next corner is a BP, owned by dear friends that you've known for years. And yes, that's the same BP that had the spill a few years ago. Which one do you choose?

Well, if it's me, there's no question. I drive the extra block and go to my friends' station, because, well... they're my friends!

Life is not just about *who you know* – life is about relationships. It is about trust, integrity, character, and honor. It's about connecting. And with the explosive growth of online and social media, anyone with a mobile phone, laptop, or library card can connect and begin to get to know you – to know your heart and your values.

And as a reader, the first thing they want to buy is *you*. They will buy into you, and then they will buy into your message. They will buy into you, and then they will buy into your brand. They will buy into you – and then they will buy your book.

Thankfully, technology has paved the way for all the connections in your life, both business and personal. There is no doubt that we live in extraordinary times... awesome, really. And yes, I know there's trouble out there as well. There's concern over prices and the economy – and education and health care and you name it. International crises pop up every so often regardless of who is in power, and every couple of years, about half of the country is seriously unhappy with the results of the latest election. But here are the positives:

1) Regardless of your point of view, those circumstances, whether exhilarating and exciting or troubling and trying, provide the seeds for a personal relationship with potentially millions of other like-minded people.

2) Whatever else is going on, never in history has it been easier or less expensive to make that connection.

Further, I believe that our level of success and happiness in any area of life – business or personal – will be determined by the quality of our relationships with other people. Since such a large part of having great relationships is frequent connection, I'm all for any new technologies, online tools, or social media and networking applications that make it easier and cheaper to do just that – with our friends, our family, or our reader.

In fourth grade, my best friend Robert moved away – far, far away it seemed, though it was just thirty-five miles. In today's currency, a telephone call at that time was about $147.58, so if it wasn't deemed an absolute emergency, it wasn't going to happen. We drifted apart and I haven't spoken to him in years, but here are two really neat developments:

1) Since then, technology has eliminated the cost factor. Many mobile plans allow for unlimited calling and messaging with no roaming charges, and there are also many online platforms available for free internet phone, chat, conferencing and video calling.

2) I just looked up Robert's professional profile online. It took me twenty seconds to get his contact info. He's married with children, living and working just south of the Twin Cities a few hours from here. How simple is that?

This is what technology does best. Through mobile communications, Internet search, long tail business models and social media, people are able to connect with others with whom they have important qualities in common. We're able to connect with our reader – and our reader with us.

Part 2

Organization

Chapter 4
Organized To Create

"I oughta write a book."
- your name here

H ere is what I believe. Regardless of your circumstances and whether you know it or not, you are blessed with exceptional and innate talents and abilities, unique strengths and insights, and special qualities and values that have the ability to connect you with other people. I also believe, whether you know it or not, that you possess life and work experiences that profoundly qualify you to write a book and enrich the lives of others.

I say, "whether you know it or not," because for many people, their own positive traits and advantages seem to be somewhat of a mystery to them. You may be one of those people – I certainly have been. And from time to time I've had the benefit of someone close to me – someone who cared enough – to set me straight.

As an example, one of the beautiful aspects of working from home and also schooling our daughter from home is that, as a family, we have shared an extraordinary amount of time together. When you don't leave each other eight to twelve hours every day of the week, you tend to engage in far more conversations with your loved ones than you would otherwise.

Frequently, during such discussions, when making a point or providing some insight or lesson, I have been told, "Now, *that* would make a great book!"

And all too often, I must tell you that my initial response was lukewarm. Many times I would think, "That doesn't seem so important," or, "Most people don't care about that," or, more commonly, "Everyone already knows that."

And almost universally, after some further discussion and a few exceptional examples from my wife, I would come to the conclusion that my insight *was* really important, that many people *do* actually care about the subject we were talking about, and no – millions of people apparently *don't* already know!

For years, Kathy has been reminding me of two very simple principles. First, we often don't recognize our own strengths, and second, even if we do, we frequently don't see anything that is all that unique or special about them.

We tend to think that if we really excel at something, everyone else must be pretty good at it too. If we see things a certain way, or understand specific subjects or concepts, we believe our understanding is the prevailing view, and it doesn't make sense to us that it would be any other way.

This is especially true with abilities that are considered natural – skills that we possess that seemed to come so easy that we didn't really have to work hard, practice, or study to attain them.

These are the subjects, habits, and activities that we're *just good at*. In many cases, we didn't have to take a course or read a stack of textbooks to learn these skills or attributes. Instead, as we grew up, we simply assimilated them from our environment in the same way that we learned to speak our first words. We didn't study these qualities or talents – one day, we just knew them. They became part of us – our identity. They're just a part of what we do and who we are.

Then, suddenly, someone notices and gives us a compliment – tells us we ought to write a book – and we respond with, "Oh, that's nothing so important... besides, everyone already knows that anyway."

A few minutes ago, I shared two principles with you that my wife often shares with me – that people often don't see their own strengths, and those that do typically reject the uniqueness of those strengths.

Now let me share another of Kathy's principles, because this is a principle that, as authors, ties our writing all together – that gives it purpose.

Here it is, in all of its simplicity: people want to know, whatever you know.

When you can weave your passion with your knowledge and experience – your strengths – you have a winning combination.

Those strengths could be anything – it matters little. It could be your ability to write terrific entertainment or poetry, or the fact that you're an amazing parent. It could be your mastery of a hobby or interest, or your expertise about any subject on Wikipedia... people are striving to do more, be more, and know more.

And they want to learn from a natural.

A few months ago, I was speaking with my brother about this book, about the publishing courses for print and Kindle, and about the doors that would be opened for countless aspiring writers and their readers.

His eyes lit up.

He confided that late one evening recently, he sat alone in his living room with pen and notepad and constructed the outline for a book that he is passionate about... a book that needs to be written and published.

I was both surprised and pleased, and I told him so. In all these years, I never knew he had the desire to write – that he had a book in him.

"Everybody has a book in them," he said. "Everybody has a story to tell."

Yes, everyone does have a story to tell. Most importantly, *you* have a story to tell. And your story has the ability to significantly impact and improve the life of another individual. I am writing to you for one purpose, and that is to inspire and organize and motivate *you* to follow your dream.

By the way, I am not writing for the whole world – I am writing for you. And I would encourage you to adopt a similar mindset.

Connect with your reader. Singular.

Write as though you're speaking to one person, teaching one person, inspiring or entertaining one person. Imagine that you are connecting with somebody that you know, and fix that image in your mind as you write. Now casually and confidently have a conversation with that individual, and capture your thoughts and words.

I learned this lesson from a good friend in the broadcasting business a few years ago, as I was about to launch into a ninety-day stint as co-host on a radio network.

Interestingly enough, it was a weekly program and we were covering Benjamin Franklin's *Thirteen Virtues,* one per week for a full three months.

In effect, Franklin's *virtues* are representative of what I referred to earlier as *values.* I believe that you may find his list to be an inspirational tool in your own writing – and also in creating your own list – so I'll post them for you at http://NewMediaJet.com/inspire along with one hundred and one others.

Now return to my story. I had never done radio before. I didn't know what I was doing, so I sought the advice and counsel of someone who did – someone with nearly thirty years experience – someone who grew up in a broadcasting studio. If he had ever written a book, I would have bought it and read it – but he didn't, so I called him on the phone.

His advice was simple.

"Quit filling the empty space with 'ums' and 'ahs,' and speak to only one listener at a time. Anyone listening should feel as though you're broadcasting just for them."

As writers, the ums and ahs are pretty easy to eliminate! But we would do well to keep in mind that the best-selling books of all time are meant to connect on an emotional level, in a personal way – one reader at a time.

To drive this home, which of the following statements impacts you more emotionally?

"Many writers are thrilled to learn that their books can finally be published."
or
"I will help you publish and sell your book on Amazon in the next 14 days!"

Your reader wants to know what they'll receive – how your knowledge and experience and wisdom can help them.

You *can* connect with the whole world – the secret is to do it by writing to an individual reader, for it is individual readers that purchase and digest your book.

As I discuss these concepts, I am often asked how to get started – how to get organized – how to pull it all together. In fact, those sentiments may be at the root of the most common questions that I hear.

For years, I have taught my employees and the others that I coach the cycle of planning, acting, and evaluating. And then the cycle simply repeats.

As authors in the creative phase, we plan (organize), we act (write), and we evaluate (edit).

So then, just how do we start? How do we pull it all together? What do we organize?

Organize Yourself

I find the whole process is much easier if I start by making sure I have myself together and organized – my thoughts, my desires, and my goals. When I really want to get something done, when I'm passionate about a cause or activity, when I truly desire a specific outcome – I am driven to put in the time or effort to do or learn what's required to make it happen.

How to do something becomes a very simple matter when it is important enough. If we want to eliminate procrastination – if we want to get started and stay started – then knowing *why* we are writing will generally lead us in the direction of *how* best to accomplish it.

Second, keeping in mind that I am ultimately writing for you – someone with whom I share common values and experience – makes it easy to connect. It is the reason why I encourage you so often and with so much energy to write from your heart – from your passion. It eliminates the need to *make up* the story, because you are *living* the story.

Elsewhere, I have stated that great relationships are the secret to a satisfying and meaningful life. They are also a key to your success as an author. One thing is for sure – it is people who buy books. If your books are to be purchased, they will be purchased by people, and that means making connections on common ground.

All relationships – business, personal, or otherwise – are fueled by common values, so where do we begin?

I suggest taking inventory – a values inventory.

Like any inventory, it is a list of what you possess at a given moment in time – it is not a wish list of things you'd like in the future. Our values are the true picture of who we are today – a snapshot of what we're really about when no one else is looking.

These values guide our actions and decisions in every area – every day of our lives. They function as a powerful rudder, settling issues before they ever arise.

And they determine both our personal and professional relationships, attracting others that share the same beliefs and qualities.

I don't know what your values are, and that's not important at the moment. What is important is that *you* know what your values are. That your family and your loved ones and your potential readers know what they are.

Start by creating a *Master Values List,* then choose the qualities and principles (values) that define you. These defining characteristics are the ones that resonate *strongly* with you – if you need to spend a great deal of time thinking about a particular one, it's probably not you.

So, if you're ready, let's go. Take out a sheet of paper and write down fifteen values, then put the list away for one hour. Because they are important components of your life, you'll identify them quickly – two or three minutes, maximum.

At the top of the next hour, and for each of the next four hours, repeat the exercise. You'll suddenly have seventy-five – the start of a great list. Total time investment – ten or fifteen minutes, tops.

Need to prime the pump?

Go to http://NewMediaJet.com/inspire and look up the *Master Values List* to begin.

With your list in hand, prioritize the principles that guide you in each area of your life – in your home, your family, your work – and in your dreams. They will be different and will hold varying degrees of relevance in your relationships and responsibilities as they guide you in the various roles that you play.

For example, in terms of importance, a value like *Perseverance* may be in your top three if you are a parent of young or teenaged children, or dealing with the stress of a physical or emotional health challenge while balancing a career as an outside salesperson in a highly competitive environment.

However, that same value may not even be in your top ten if you're sailing through your job as a bank teller or member of an accounts payable team where values such as *Trust, Courtesy,* and *Attention To Detail* are the critical values for success.

Similarly, many may overlap – *Loyalty, Kindness, Communication, Honesty, Creativity,* and *Teamwork* may be integral for your marriage and family relationships, as well as other important areas of your life or business. The goal is to define the handful of most important values that guide your decisions, actions, and relations with others – and then drive them deep. These are the non-negotiables in your life – the place where your legacy is formed, your reputation is forged, and your connections with your reader solidified.

It's where the real work of purpose-filled relationships begin. As authors, through this simple exercise we are given the insight and ability to line up our subject matter with our values, and our writing suddenly takes on impact and meaning.

Further, identifying your most important values could easily provide you with ideas for your next several books, articles, or eBooks.

Organize Your Time

Years ago, I remember my dad giving me some advice regarding time and priorities.

"Steve," he said, "if you're looking for someone who can get things done, talk to the busiest person you know. If it's a worthwhile project, they'll figure out a way to fit it in. Everyone else – especially those who accomplish the least – well, they just never seem to have any time."

I've seen this concept proven with authors and leaders over and over again. The ones with the most to do – those who live on purpose – tend to become experts in prioritizing their life. They do what they need to do, and you must do the same.

I'm not saying that these people are always willing to jam eighteen more things into their day, but they consistently make time for the *really important* things. And they aren't often sidelined by activities that come out of left field.

On the other hand, we all know people who are seemingly tossed by the waves – by the expectations of others, by pop culture, and by peer pressure. Their lives are ruled by their boss, their mother, their children's teachers, and the TV Guide.

Then opportunity knocks, or missions call – the chance of a lifetime awaits. And the calls are answered by silence. Unfortunately, these folks are often too busy to notice, or too tired to care. In fact, most often they don't even realize what just passed them by.

I was asked last week by an up-and-coming writer how he can do a better job of managing his time while he looks to grow his brand and increase his influence and credibility through writing and publishing.

In addition to working a full-time career in the corporate world, he is also a health advocate, and wants to start an online business marketing nutrition and wellness products. His ultimate goal is to use this additional influence and credibility to expand his following, generate additional leads, and close more sales.

I cover *Influence* and *Credibility* in Chapter 6, but I'll summarize the time component of our discussion here.

My first question to him was one I've asked hundreds of people over the years:

"Do you know how much time you have – specifically, how many total hours are there in a week?"

Off the top of his head, he didn't know – most don't.

This young man started to do some quick math, but then defaulted to telling me about his standard work week –

which was about 55 hours, including his commute. So we went back to the math and worked out the numbers together.

Not surprisingly, he found that there were 168 hours in his week – every week – the same as in yours and mine. Subtracting his work and commute he had 113 left. He determined that he spent 19 hours per week between eating and hygiene, another 5 on exercise, and 49 sleeping.

That left him with 40 hours every week to use or invest in whatever was important to him.

I suggested that he take 60% of it (24 hours) and invest it in his family and relationships. This extra time also allows for a buffer if he needs it. I then proposed that he take the remaining 40% (16 hours) and invest it in a writing, marketing, and business plan that could replace his income in the next 3-5 years.

He opted to reverse the numbers, and replace his full-time job in 2-3 years instead.

You can do the same.

Organize Your Space

Somewhere in my youth, I saw some old black and white photographs of an author at work. Crumpled sheets of paper overflowed a small metal trash container, littering the floor around him as he sat at a solitary desk in the middle of a large and dimly lit library on the third story of his retreat, surrounded by books – his own and others'.

At the time, I imagined it was quiet. I assumed it was late. And to this day, it is the stereotype I have in my mind. It is not, however, the view you'd have of me in my office if you could see me right now.

As I write, I am seated in the most comfortable chair in our home, reclined back a few inches with my feet up on a small footstool and my keyboard on my lap.

My monitor is just in front of me on a sixty-inch table that is also home to my desktop tower, some really terrific speakers, a scanner and an ink jet printer.

This spare room has been converted into an office for three people – my wife, my daughter, and me – and though sometimes a very busy environment, with foam plugs in my ears, I am completely free of distractions as my fingers hit the keys about as fast as they ever do!

It's bright – very bright, in fact, not dimly lit at all – and the space is fairly crowded, with a built-in desk and work area that houses a second desktop, a laptop, and all of our records and files.

Some people work best in pristine environments – others not. I'm in the middle. Many years ago, I had a boss who looked at my desk and commented that a cluttered desk meant a cluttered mind. He wasn't sure how to respond when I asked him what an empty desk meant.

Would I like more space? Absolutely. Do I believe I'll have more in the future? Count on it. But for now, I don't use it as a reason to procrastinate. I make it work, and that's all that's important.

I also have alternate places to write – a park with a beautiful view of the river, a library with west-facing windows on the second floor that overlook the same river, and a scenic parking area by our airport, the same airport where I earned my private pilot certificate.

These are places that I am comfortable, and having access to the web anywhere and anytime eliminates the need for many other physical resources in the environment.

Dictionary? It's online.

Thesaurus? That's online too.

Citations for crediting the work of others? Google.

Grammar? That's the one small book in front of me.

Of course, I could easily find a decent grammar site on the web also, but I happen to have a terrific book that I actually enjoy – *Painless Grammar* by Rebecca Elliot, Ph.D. – that answers 95% of my questions quickly and understandably, and I hit the Internet for the rest.

So find your comfortable place, open multiple tabs on your browser for the resources that you need, and begin creating.

Organize Your Work

Earlier, I shared that the most frequent set of questions I receive on this topic has to do with pulling it all together.

Frequently, people have ideas racing through their minds a mile a minute. They have pieces here and pieces there, in journals and notebooks – on scraps of paper. Many have been writing for years, never considering the possibility of getting published. And suddenly technology revolutionizes the industry and all of their dreams come back!

"I oughta write a book," they say!

Then, unfortunately and all too often, fear and doubt creep in as they struggle with the idea of pulling it all together. They're already stretched thin – trying to multitask their way through each day – and putting an unknown, like writing, into the mix pushes them to the edge.

Thankfully, the answer is easier than it seems and well within their reach – and yours.

The first step is to eliminate the myth of multitasking. Regardless of how spread out you are, no matter how many piles your book is in, you will pull your book together one piece at a time.

The term multitasking came into favor a number of years ago when computers advanced to running different programs and processes concurrently. Some managers suddenly thought that it would be great if people could be more like computers, and the expectation of you becoming a multitasker was born.

In reality, the term refers to the ability to juggle a lot of different responsibilities, activities, or decisions within a condensed period of time, or the stability to handle a great deal of stress or pressure at once. The truth is that we *are not* multitaskers. We work on one thing at a time, we think about one thing at a time, and we write one thing at a time.

For example, I am not writing this sentence in this paragraph and another in Chapter 7 at the same time. I might like to do that, but it just isn't so. I can toggle back and forth – I can reduce the time spent in each section to a miniscule amount – but I am giving my *full and focused attention* to one thing at a time.

Here, try this exercise: count backwards from the number ten, out loud. Go ahead – ten, nine, eight, seven, six, five, four, three, two, one, zero.

Very good, now do it again – but this time, I want you to do something that would be elementary for a multitasking computer to do: when you get to seven, also begin reciting your ABC's at exactly the same time. Ready, set, go! We're not computers – nor are we true multitaskers.

The second step in pulling it all together is to break each activity down into smaller and smaller components.

The rule is straightforward. If you're trying to deal with completely diverse sections, concepts, or ideas in your book – break them down into like-parts. If you are attempting to write, edit, and publish at the same time – you have gotten ahead of yourself. And if you are feeling overwhelmed by it all – you are.

Overwhelm is a symptom that what is on your plate is too big to be handled as is. Break it down. Cut it in half – then cut it in half again. Commit to completing one section at a time, whatever that happens to be for you. Often, that may mean working on one chapter or one sub-chapter. At other times, it may be just one page, one paragraph, or one idea.

Remind yourself why writing this book is important. Visualize the people who will be buying your book and receiving the benefits of your work. Picture yourself bringing a copy of your new book to your workplace, hot off the presses, or giving it to your friends or members of your family.

As you push through and complete one section at a time, you get stronger – each obstacle becomes smaller, each challenge weaker. And it all begins with dividing up the task into bites that you can manage.

In writing our book, we begin with a purpose – a goal, a reason to write. Why are we writing? What do we want our reader to receive? What would we like him or her to learn, to experience, to feel, to believe, to think, or to do?

You see, the first step is not to write a book – the first step is to connect with yourself and decide why you want to write it to begin with. Why is it important, and what benefit can you offer? If you really are struggling here, go back to the basics – go to your *Values Inventory.*

Next, pull together your writings, old letters, and blog posts. Look at the types of conversations you have in social networking environments, or the notes you take in meetings at work. These tend to reflect the subjects, ideas, or qualities that you value.

What are you good at? What do you enjoy? What do you get passionate about – or angry about? What kind of advice do people tend to ask you for? What problems have you solved? How would your friends describe you? What would you spend your hundred thousand dollars on?

Once decided, we simply ask questions that break it down into parts that we believe are necessary to achieving our objective for writing. This exercise reveals a rough outline, which is worked and shaped and becomes, one day, a defined Table of Contents.

The day you settle on your Table of Contents is like freedom day. It just feels right. You're in the groove and you know it. It is the butterfly emerging from the cocoon – a thing of beauty.

Here's a tip: if you don't feel it, you're not quite there yet. Allow me to share the actual construction of this book.

It began simply enough with New Media Jet's publication of several books for others – books that had been in the works for years. I referenced one of these projects in the introductory chapter.

As I shared the stories of getting these books published, men and women from every walk of life began to reach out and offer their own hopes and dreams of leaving something behind. Of improving their world. Of leaving a legacy. One after another told of wanting to write *their* book.

Ninety days ago, I returned home late one evening and sat down at my desk. It had been an extraordinary day, with several exceptional interactions. Without thinking, I created the following document – a document which I have read every day since, and which graces my desk within arm's reach this very minute:

Two great conversations today.
One gentleman is eighty-six – the other, eighty.

Rarely shown and often hidden deeply,
many of these powerful men are just longing
to know that their lives still matter,
that their work still impacts,
that their experience is valuable,
and that they are loved, appreciated, and important right now.

They want to know that they're not done.

When you're with them you can see it,
on the telephone you can hear it,
when you walk away you can feel it.

And it breathes both life and purpose into them –
and into me.

– Steve Buelow

The following morning, I shared my words with Kathy, and the vision was born. That deeply-hidden feeling that these individuals expressed, that longing to have life matter, to make an impact, to be of value and importance – to be loved and appreciated now – is common to each of us.

As we have discussed, I believe everyone has a book in them – a story to tell – but the price tag, among other things, has always held them back. Just the day before, I had sent out quotes for two potential projects – one for writing and the other for publishing. The first was $15,600 and the second was $9,200. Such fees have for years kept millions of people from having their written works published. Many others never even put their words and ideas to paper because they believed they could never afford to have their works in print.

As my wife and I spoke and the ideas developed, we were excited that we might change the entire game for all of them – and for you. Kathy was in the zone – it's a place where good things happen for others.

"Steve, you need to write a book! All of these people have a story. They don't know they could be published. The technology's there, they can do this, and you can teach them!"

And, of course, she was right.

On that morning, there were *two initial objectives:*

1) We wanted to inspire, organize, and motivate you to write – to breathe the kind of life and purpose back into your spirit that I experienced with those two gentlemen on the previous page. This desire on our part flows from a sincere and powerful belief that you are destined to be a gift in someone's life whom you've likely never met, and the answer to the prayers that they will pray tonight.

2) Book publishing is a straightforward but often daunting process that keeps many terrific and promising authors on the sidelines. This need not be. We wanted to provide you with a *step-by-step, click-by-click* guide – literally from cover to cover – allowing you to professionally and independently publish, distribute, *and profit* from your work in 30 days or less.

Two simple objectives. Just one challenge – they don't belong in the same book. The first objective is inspirational. The second, a very intensive how-to manual. Profoundly unique styles, distinctly different genres.

In fact, as we developed the outline, it quickly became apparent that the second objective really doesn't belong in a book *at all* – at least not in this century.

Today it belongs on video.

It is powerful and effective as an interactive course. The content thrives in an online community or member environment where changes and upgrades can be digitally delivered at the speed of thought, and without further cost to the reader or member.

The entire publishing process – from start to finish – is not easily *described*. It is, however, *very easily demonstrated,* especially on video where you can simply follow along – watch, and do.

And, if necessary, watch again.

Just imagine if this book were suddenly much bigger, say 8½ x 11 inches, and maybe an additional four or five hundred pages – all with hundreds and hundreds of similar-looking, black and white screenshots that all just sort of blended together and put you to sleep after twenty minutes.

Imagine trying to keep your interest, or your place, as you worked back and forth.

What a nightmare!

Indeed, what would have started with a fast-paced and inspirational read about your dreams and your vision and your power and ability to influence would suddenly have wound its way into a long and – dare I say – boring technical manual that could not possibly be delivered with the same level of excellence.

So we broke it down. Writing is your *first* step – publishing is your *next* step. This book was written to inspire, organize, and motivate you to write.

Then we designed an easy-to-follow video course to help simplify the publishing process for both books and eBooks, avoid costly mistakes, and allow you to publish and distribute your works nationally and internationally within 30 days – in fact, as little as seven days.

You can learn more about making money from home and publishing books and eBooks for yourself and others by visiting http://NewMediaJet.com/publish and check out the courses created just for you.

As this book came together we made one *global decision,* and I suggest you do the same. When you're ready, you will discover this important component by asking yourself the following question: *what do I want my reader to do, think, or experience because they read my book?*

It could be anything – anything important to you. It is the reason that you are writing, that you are offering your wisdom and knowledge, your strengths and insights, your laughter and joy, your tears and pain, your humor and hope.

Everything rises and falls on the answer you receive.

From there, each part, chapter, and sub-chapter are simply broken out into workable parts of a few hundred words at a time and then reassembled to make a whole. If you are a journalist or a blogger, you may be pleasantly surprised to find out how much of your book has already been written for you.

Gather your writings together, organize them by topic, and use them, when and where appropriate, to construct your outline.

For example, the global decision made for *Your Time To Shine* was simple – I want you to *write your book,* and I want you to do it *now.*

I want you to act on your vision, your passion, your dreams – without delay – now.

And that, in my opinion, is best achieved if you are inspired, organized, and motivated. Are you seeing the outline of this book develop here? Within hours there were several refinements, and suddenly the Table of Contents began to emerge:

Introduction
Part 1: Inspiration
Part 2: Organization
Part 3: Motivation
Epilogue

How simple was that?

Next, we broke down the three parts into chapters, and the chapters into the sub-chapters that you are reading this very minute. You can do this too, by beginning with your global decision.

So just what *are* you going to write about?

What is your global decision? What do you want your reader to do, think, or experience because they read your book? And when will you have your manuscript written and published?

Make a decision, make a commitment to start.

If you're still looking for ideas on where to begin, visit http://NewMediaJet.com/inspire, for one hundred and one exceptional topic ideas that will get you writing today.

Organize Your Process

I believe that one of the reasons that many goals and dreams are missed is because they are not scheduled – the process isn't organized.

Years ago, I had a mentor who asked about my vision for the future. This was a question I thought about relentlessly. I could describe it in minute detail. When I closed my eyes, I could see it clearly.

And then he stopped me.

"What is the date... the date that it will be yours?"

I didn't know. I didn't *have* a date. Just a dream – a vision. He chuckled as he said that without a deadline, it was likely not a vision – but an hallucination. I also seem to remember that, at the time, he seemed to think that was significantly funnier than I did.

But he was right.

Writing and publishing may have some complexities to them, but as we have spoken about, they can be broken down into smaller and smaller components – bite-size processes – that can easily be completed one at a time, just like you do daily in your career now, or have done in any job you have ever held in the past.

When I speak with budding authors who just haven't found the time to write, they often express sentiments like, "I don't understand why this is taking so long... I've been wanting to do this for years! I'm so productive at work... why can't I get this done?"

Well, there may be a number of answers for that, and we covered many causes of procrastination in Chapter 2. However, it may be no more difficult than this: it may not be getting done, because it isn't organized to get done.

You see, on a job – in a business or company – the work is organized. The day is organized, schedules are organized, people and processes and tasks are organized.

Even if you think your company is different and that it is very disorganized, one thing is certain – it is organized enough that the most critical steps are being completed, or else the business would not survive.

Further, on the opposite side of the organization coin is responsibility and accountability. Once the nature of the business is organized, you are given some responsibility to contribute to the big picture – to ensure that the products or services are being designed and produced and delivered and paid for.

In other words, the whole has been broken down, organized, and scheduled, and the necessary energy has been applied to complete each piece.

But what happens when we go home, when we have many other responsibilities that we are juggling, with children or parents or health concerns, when our time is our own – or when we are overwhelmed or exhausted? What happens to our dream, our vision, our goals, and our creativity then? What happens to the book we decided to write?

If we don't break it down, don't schedule it, and don't put in the necessary energy, one thing is for certain: it is not going to write itself, and the publishing will have to wait.

Earlier in this chapter, we spoke of organizing and prioritizing time. I have never met anyone in my life who could not find time or make time for the things that were most important in their life.

If an emergency situation arises, we make time. We cancel other plans, rearrange, whatever. I encourage you to put a priority on your vision and invest at least a fraction of the time that you currently give to achieving the desires of others into achieving the desires of your own heart.

In completing your book, you will likely want to organize your ideas and your time around the following activities:
1) Researching your subject, genre, and market.
2) Collecting your thoughts and resources.
3) Writing your outline, draft, and final manuscript.
4) Editing your work with the help of others.
5) Crediting your sources or helps.
6) Publishing your work professionally and
   independently.
7) Marketing and selling your amazing new book!

The key in this process is to show up for work. If you were hired to do a job for someone else, you'd arrange the time in your calendar and be present to perform your responsibilities as agreed.

Do the same for yourself.

Make appointments with yourself in your calendar and clear out the time to work on activities that will bring you the life you deserve and desire. Then when the phone rings or you receive an invitation to go here or there, first check your calendar. If it is clear, go for it! However, if you have scheduled time for yourself and your project, it becomes a simple matter to say, "Thanks, I appreciate the invite... but I'll be working."

Everyone understands that, and it'll take you from the creation stage to the publication stage to the marketing stage faster than you've ever imagined.

Chapter 5
Organized To Connect

"Do unto others, as you would have them do to you."
- The Golden Rule

You know you can write – you've always known you could write. That isn't a concern, and you're also not worried about the publishing process anymore, because we can easily walk you step-by-step through that.

No, for many authors, writing and publishing aren't the issue – it's what happens *after* the writing and publishing that hangs them up.

Some call it sales and are intimidated by the process. Some call it marketing and are unsure where to begin. I call it connecting with your world – one person or organization at a time – and I believe it's what we were put on this earth to do.

Let's remove the sales and marketing labels for just a minute and look at what's really going on.

Regardless of the genre you prefer, the challenges and opportunities you will likely experience in writing, publishing, and marketing your book are quite similar in many respects to those faced by small business owners everywhere – and every day. In fact, writing and publishing this new book of yours may be your very first step into the environment of self-employment and free enterprise.

Pretty exciting – especially once things start moving!

But questions abound. How do you identify your ideal customer? What are the common denominators between your readers? Where do they live and work? What are their most pressing concerns, and how does your product – your knowledge, your solution, your creation, your book – help them move closer to whatever they are seeking to move closer to right now?

More importantly, how do you reach them, how do you meet them – how do you connect?

In the past, this connection process could be very difficult, very time-consuming, and very expensive. Traditional marketing, sales, and media channels were theoretically available to all – as long as you could pay the price tag.

Most couldn't... and most *still* can't today.

When I opened my first business in the mid-1980's, I was told I would have to do big media buys on television and radio in order to compete and survive.

I couldn't afford it, so I marketed our services the only way I knew how – by connecting with people personally and forming relationships. Yes, we made cold calls and printed brochures. Yes, we did trade shows, and we got press wherever we could get it. But most importantly, we delivered the results that our customers were seeking.

We asked for referrals. We networked.

There were many appointments – and many disappointments – but our business grew, our products and services sold, and that is exactly what will happen for you today! Now, please be aware that as you begin to grow, as your brand becomes more powerful, as your book begins to sell, you will have people come out of the woodwork to try and get you to part with a good percentage of your royalties by making unplanned purchases of media time or online and offline marketing/training courses.

Don't fall for it. While I do believe that some training and most media and advertising outlets are valuable for one purpose or another, here is an absolute fact: most of them are *likely not* the best choice for marketing and selling your book. Also, remember that when you are on the receiving end of a spontaneous offer from an organization or agency by phone, e-mail, social networking ad, or otherwise, the representative on the other end is trying to meet their own production goals, not yours.

One of the common challenges you face as an author (small business owner) is that there's no limit to the number of activities and options that can stretch your marketing resources and whatever limited budget you may have. The opportunities and channels to market your books are everywhere. Let's focus on three essential considerations:

1) Most importantly, your marketing must be planned. As fundamental as this sounds, many authors do not have a proactive marketing plan that is tied to a specific set of strategies, and that is subordinate to a calendar and budget. This allows for many marketing surprises, and the temptation to engage in unplanned media or training buys that come literally out of nowhere. This is especially true today with the explosion of social media advertising.

2) As true as it is that "not every idea is a good idea," it's even more important to understand that "not every *good* idea is the *best* idea." A bad idea often carries little danger, because it's so obvious – everyone can see that it's a bad idea! But *good* ideas

are different. Because they make sense, they can keep us from digging deeper and seeing what would have been the *best* course of action – and they often steal energy and necessary financial resources. Keep in mind that in marketing, the best idea is the one that accomplishes a very specific objective with the *least* amount of stress on whatever resource is required.

3) As effective as traditional marketing channels may have been, new media technologies have dramatically altered the marketing landscape and our ability to connect. Not only are they incredibly cost-effective, they also provide a level of reader engagement that was incomprehensible in the past. Most importantly – and please do not miss this – they have leveled the playing field.

When thinking of both traditional and new media marketing, it is also important to keep in mind that the explosion of technology has altered the way we respond to offers, and the way we want to be interacted with.

We want our space. For example, how often do people look at their Caller ID before deciding whether to answer the phone? What percentage of U.S. households are on the "Do Not Call" list? Are you or anyone you know on that list?

As we are inundated with advertising 24-7, studies show that consumers increasingly distrust the message, and even resent the advertisers for interrupting their chosen activity.

Why is TiVo popular? Or satellite radio or pop-up blockers or spam filters? When it comes to information, we want *what* we want. But we also want it *when* we want it.

Now here's the shift.

Because of exceptional technology and access to accurate and unlimited search, we feel confident in our ability to find information ourselves, in the peace and comfort of our own homes, on our mobile devices, on our own schedules, and from sources that we trust.

Yet, here's the neat thing.

As technology has increased our ability to retreat and to insulate ourselves from people and processes and environments that we *don't* like, as social beings we still want to be around people and processes and environments that we *do* like.

We want decent relationships, with decent people. And your reader wants a relationship with you. How cool is that!

As an author, the timing could not be better, for your ability to use social media allows you to easily connect with those with whom you have important qualities in common. Further, as it establishes relationships that enable you to focus on meeting the true needs of your reader, it improves the effectiveness of all the other communications you may have with that person through chat or e-mail or even live or call-in seminars as your audience grows.

Over one million people opened a social networking account last week. I believe that some of them would like to read your book!

Organize Your Approach – A Little Respect

I received a private message on Facebook last week from a woman in New York City. We had a brief chat online, during which she sent several questions.

How long had I been working in the health and nutrition field? What were my results? Was I open to a conversation? Would I look at an eight-minute video that her company had produced, and was I willing to give her some feedback regarding her current marketing plan?

Here is my answer, cut and pasted – verbatim:

"Thank you for being so respectful... you may send a link to me, Laurel, and I look forward to hearing of your continuing success – Steve"

She did what she said she would do and followed up with the link and a phone number. I did what I said I would do by watching the video and then making myself available for an appointment. We had a delightful conversation, found we have several important qualities in common, and the door is open for the future.

It began with respect.

I appreciated that and told her so. She responded by quoting the Golden Rule. Now contrast Laurel's approach to others (unaffiliated with her) in the same firm.

In the two or three weeks prior to our conversation, I had received hundreds of unsolicited offers from other independent contractors in the company. A few added me to their groups and then spammed me several times per hour. Several tagged me in photos which then posted to my photo stream.

No big deal, but it looked like an endorsement – which I hadn't given. Others thought it was cool to just use my wall without permission to advertise to *my* friends directly.

The mistake they were making, of course, is that they were applying old rules of advertising to new technologies in media. They were engaging in something known in the past as "mass marketing."

I received the most intriguing voicemail some time back. The caller had read an article I had written somewhere on this very subject, and was making a case against the effectiveness of using the Internet and social networking for any type of business or marketing.

In fact, in his estimation, *all* Internet marketing is mass marketing, and he wanted to make the point that:

1) Mass marketing is a waste of time.

2) Mass marketing is a waste of money.

3) Mass marketing doesn't create personal relationships.

Of course, as I define mass marketing – an attempt to cater to all needs, wants, or desires through a singular offer, message, or strategy – I would agree with those three points. I would also add that mass marketing, again as I define it, doesn't create much of a relationship with your brand, either!

The reason is simple.

Any attempt to market to everyone will undeniably water down your content, and likely the quality of your product or service as well. One size rarely fits all.

But that's not what was so interesting to me.

No, what interested me was that the caller could identify the *negative use* of social media in reaching a target audience, but could not imagine a *positive use* or process for creating the type of relationships or loyalty that could transfer to the business side. To him, all Internet marketing was mass marketing, and consisted only of spamming tens of thousands of people in an effort to have a few buy whatever product it was that the company was hawking. You know – it's the tired old idea about throwing enough mud on the wall. Any such approach used online will continue to generate the same pathetic results as it always has offline – plus the added negative today of just plain ticking off people who hate spam!

* PLEASE NOTE *
Ticking people off is a universally lousy marketing strategy.

But the assertion that the Internet is nothing more than just another broadcast channel is to miss its significance entirely. The Web, and especially mobile technology, is all about connecting with others just like ourselves, who value the same principles, and with whom we share a common bond.

These threads wind their way through our lives and thoughts and relationships, and as authors, they become identifiers of our ideal market – in other words, our niche.

And in our niche, it is all about the relationship, all about transparency, all about getting to know our reader, and really letting them get to know us.

You see, if they get to know us well enough, they may actually begin to like us, and then to trust us. Heck, they might even fall in love with us! And, at that point, it is completely possible that they may consider buying from us, and ultimately promoting us. Imagine that.

This voice message revealed to me how ingrained concepts can often stick with us even when they no longer make contextual sense. Here was an individual who has been in the business world for decades, but who was still hanging on to a preconceived notion about an old technology, and applying it – with force – to a new and wonderful and freeing technology that has the potential to make the world a more humane and connected place.

What's more, this gentleman happens to be a leader within an organization that recently announced their decision to target almost $500,000,000 to big media traditional branding and advertising campaigns of the sort that were popular at the height of the Merchandising and Advertising ages decades ago.

The kind that stands on the sidelines and shouts loudly, that interrupts your programming at every commercial break to push their message on you whether you're interested or not. The kind with no respect – in other words, mass marketing.

Organize Your Attitude – It's No Longer Just "Who You Know"

Last evening, I was waiting in line at the grocery store when suddenly, from behind, a familiar saying hit my ears: "Well, like they say, it ain't *what* you know, it's *who* you know."

Now, it may just be me, but I am always suspicious about anything that anonymous people named "they" say, even if what "they" say has wound its way into the very fabric of our American psyche and is accepted by the majority to be gospel.

It's not that the saying doesn't have some truth to it – most sayings *became* sayings for the fundamental reason that they could be demonstrated in various circumstances. And certainly, within the literary and publishing world of the past, *who you knew* did matter.

When there were only a handful of agents and executives that controlled the industry, knowing the right people could definitely be a major plus in the advancement of your work or career as a writer.

But it was *never* the *only* thing that mattered.

To be sure, *what you know* has always been important, and is even more so today. Your expertise combined with today's technology and your ability to write, connect, and influence will give you all the contacts you need. If you want to sell books and make an impact in *this* century, the most important connections you have are with your reader, and others of influence who can introduce you to more readers.

In fact, therein lies the major flaw with the "ain't what you know, but who you know" argument.

It's the wrong attitude.

The individual is saying that they have the skills; they just don't have the relationships. If they only knew who *you* knew, they'd be further along. And whether or not it was ever true in the past, here is the truth right now:

You have the ability this very day to connect with someone who will buy your book, and that person likely knows a hundred others in their social network. Each of the individuals are similarly connected with a hundred more – some even thousands more – and on and on and on.

The progression goes from 1 to 100 to 10,000 to 1,000,000 and beyond. You don't need to be a math major to see the potential, and you don't need to sell a million books to be successful. Take an $8 royalty on each of 10,000 books and tell me if it would change anything in your life in the next 3-6 months.

You see, it's not that difficult to meet people who are

engaged and influential. They tend to hang around other engaged and influential people – people like you. And as you will see in the next chapter, writing and publishing a book is one of the fastest paths to influence that you can imagine.

Further, in the age of social media, there is now a turnabout. It is no longer just what you know, or who you know – it's also who knows you, and what they know about you. Of course, what they know about you is what you choose to let them know about you – what information you share with them or present to them.

Lee Iacocca, the legendary executive with Ford and Chrysler, is reported by John Maxwell to have said that success comes from who you know, and also how you present yourself to each of those people.

In the beginning, it's the first impression, and we all know that "you only get one chance to make a first impression."

So it must be important.

But then we also hear that, "First impressions can be misleading," and that, "Things aren't always what they seem," and certainly, "You can't judge a book by its cover."

Still, as our relationships progress, we must continue to present ourselves and our ideas to others, and how we do that certainly matters. So, it's time for a quiz: in terms of real, sustainable relationships with others, and success in your career, which is most important?

a) What you know
b) Who you know (and who knows you)
c) How you present yourself to (b)
d) All of the above
e) None of the above

Before you answer, may I offer you one last thought that will lead to what I believe is the most critical element? It's not that I disagree that any of these components are important, but I believe that this formula for success is just too limited.

While smarts, or smart packaging, may get you in the door, over the long haul, enough tough stuff will show up to strip off the paint and reveal what's inside. That's when character attributes like perseverance, stability, honesty, selflessness, dependability, loyalty, courage and trust will carry you to victory. It is also when the lack of these characteristics will sink your ship.

That fact is another reason why I had you create a *Values Inventory* in the previous chapter – to give you a good idea of your strengths, as well as areas that you may want to work to strengthen. I will return to that topic in the following section as well.

True success is based on relationships, and relationships are built on long-term interactions of one sort or another between individuals who have many common qualities, ideas, and beliefs in the areas that matter to them most.

So, I believe that the answer to the quiz is, (e) None of the above. And I will rewrite what I hope will one day be an even more popular saying:

"True success in your relationships and career comes *not only* from what you know, and who you know... but most importantly from *who you are*."

Organize Your Assets

We began the chapter by acknowledging that while many authors have no trouble once they get started writing, they do worry a great deal about the steps that come after the writing is complete – the sales and marketing. I stated that I believe the answer lies in creating relationships – connecting with your world – and I'll expand on that process now. The truth is that relationships *naturally* develop between people who share common experiences, missions, beliefs, and priorities. These characteristics form our core values, and we attract – and are attracted by – others with whom we have singleness of purpose.

Note that I said the relationships develop naturally. When we stop pushing, we attract to us exactly what we are, for better or worse. As an author, you are the brand. It is *your* book – conceived in your heart, influenced by your beliefs, and stamped with your approval. It will attract others who seek similar answers, experience similar joy, possess a similar sense of humor, and live by similar values.

This is another great use for your *Values Inventory*. The results can clearly define your market, and may be used to frame your arguments, your passion, and topics you may wish to consider for future writing. May I suggest that if you haven't already done so, take a break and complete it now. On the deepest, most personal level, identify the traits and qualities that are most important to you. Write them down.

This isn't up for a vote. It needn't be shown to anyone else. Nor should it be swayed by public opinion. This is about you, and what inspires and motivates you – what will drive you to expand your influence and positively impact as many others as possible.

If you're like many writers, you may already have a pretty good source to turn to in putting this inventory together – a source which also doubles as a potentially significant reservoir of enthusiastic buyers for your book, even if you haven't written it yet. Look at your blog, and if you don't have a blog, consider creating one today.

There are many advantages to writing online. Among others, blogging will:

1) Instill a habit of writing consistently.
2) Sharpen your creative talents.
3) Improve your decision-making and research skills.
4) Focus you in areas of interest and passion.
5) Provide the potential for multiple revenue streams.

More importantly for this section, blogging will:

6) Integrate easily with your social networks.
7) Attract readership from individuals with common ideas, beliefs and values.
8) Allow individual readers to contribute.
9) Offer you the ability to sell your book in your own store, on your own site.

And the price is right – it costs little or next to nothing. In fact, it actually *can be* done for nothing, though I do not recommend that option. You'll find a free download of WordPress at http://NewMediaJet.com/inspire, along with some terrific places for low-cost (even free) images for your blog, and options for significantly-discounted hosting packages that will have you up and running in no time.

In advising others who are beginning to write, this is often the starting ground. Many aspiring authors have found that, piece by piece, they had previously organized and produced so much content regarding a particular interest or topic that they had much of their book already written.

Several years ago, I had ghostwritten a series of 57 articles for a counselor in the medical field. Some were sent as press releases. Others were reprinted in newspapers, newsletters, and magazines. All were published on his blog.

It was this activity, publishing the articles on his blog, that really made an impact in his practice. Readership on all pages of his website went up as his search ranking climbed and his credibility increased.

Suddenly, requests for a book began to come in. So we wrote one. The work I had done the previous year totally laid the groundwork. I had covered the subject so thoroughly through the writing of a simple article each week, that the book seemed to write itself.

Simple.

Another approach is to blog the entire book as it is written, allowing individual readers to contribute. Comments can be received publicly or privately and included in the creative process.

What are the chances that a reader will buy your book if they know that their contribution – their story or ideas – are included and credited properly? My guess is that they'll buy several copies – one or two for themselves, and a few to give away.

Doesn't get much easier than that.

Of course, you can also just simply publish your blog articles as is. In *Small Is the New Big: and 183 Other Riffs, Rants, and Remarkable Business Ideas*, author and thinker extraordinaire, Seth Godin, did just that. He took a collection of his most popular posts and articles from his blog and turned them into a bestseller. These strategies, known as re-purposing, contain the seeds of significant economies of scale, and can also be used for the creation of peripheral and complementary products and services. We'll speak further of this in Part 3.

Organize Your Connections

In speaking about connecting with others through authenticity and common values, we don't want to miss the opportunities available through your social networks or the blogs and writings of others.

Take a look at the places you visit online, the sites you have made favorites, the people you friend, follow, or include in your circles. Be aware of the ties that bind, the conversations you have, or – more importantly – the conversations you could be having.

It is as simple a matter to search blogs for common areas of interest as it is to search the rest of the web. Articles posted on blogs are indexed by the search engines just as any other content, and even more often, in many cases, because blog content tends to be more dynamic – it tends to be updated more often.

And that means you can organize some time in your day or your week to connect and to comment – to begin a conversation – on the blog of someone else with whom you share interests or values. For starters, just ten minutes will do.

I'll guarantee you'll find someone just like you. Someone who wants to know that their ideas are valuable, that they can change and improve circumstances just by the way they think and write.

So imagine stumbling across this person's blog tomorrow morning: for the past six months, they've been consistently and loyally sharing their most personal thoughts and ideas, brainstorming solutions to whatever need they believe needs solving, completely clarifying and organizing their thoughts, outlining their story and tracking the entire concept through to a logical and powerful conclusion, and then publishing their recommendations on their new blog that, as far as they can tell...

No one else is reading.

Day after day after week after week... and then, suddenly, you show up and leave a comment, an insight, a genuine compliment! It may be their very first one! They may call someone, take a screenshot or a picture – who knows what!

But they will be excited, because they are not alone.

I once wrote an article called *Give or Take*.

A few days earlier, several friends and I were riding together and, while parked at a stoplight, I glanced over and noticed a beautifully restored classic car next to us at the intersection. It was spotless – no, it was flawless. The maroon-and-cream-colored paint was as thick as the chrome that coated the bumpers on each end, and the window frames and mirrors in between.

It must have cost a small fortune in dollars and an even greater investment in time, energy and passion. One look at the driver and you could sense the emotion – the pride – the desire to be noticed and acknowledged. At once, I rolled down my window, threw my thumb into the air, and exclaimed, "That is absolutely beautiful – awesome!"

You should have seen his face – he was beaming.

Minutes down the road, we were approaching a line of cars that were traveling far too slowly for that particular stretch of highway. As I moved to the fast lane, I suddenly realized that there were several more vintage automobiles in the group, each as incredible in their detail as was the first a few miles earlier.

Without even thinking, I slowed as I passed each one, nodding approval to each driver as we made eye contact. Those men who were accompanied by women seemed especially proud, as if the added attention from me somehow justified that the money invested and the years of intense labor and commitment had all been worth it.

I wanted nothing from any of them – to be sure, I would likely never see any of them again. At that moment, one friend riding with me asked, "What year was that car?" (I had no idea.) Another asked about the make and model (I had no clue), and then followed up with, "Gosh, Steve, I never knew you were so interested in old cars."

"Don't know the first thing about them," I said. "I just know beauty and hard work and commitment when I see it, and I know that people need to be acknowledged."

Over the years, I can't tell you how many times I've suggested to others that the next words out of their mouth could lift up or knock down, encourage or harm, create or destroy. I also can't even venture a guess as to how many times I've come to regret the choices I've made in this regard.

I believe the truth is that the *life-givers* are far outnumbered by the *energy-takers*, and that a kind word from you, or an unconditional act of support, encouragement, or approval may be the only one that an individual receives that day, that week, or in what seems like forever.

You see, the cars were just cars. They mattered only because the people that were in them mattered. As you begin to connect with your world, you will find many such circumstances. The creativity and the art, the blogs and the book, all matter because the creator matters.

Ask yourself these questions:

1) Do you know people whom others just love to be around? What are the attributes that define them?
2) Do you know others who drain emotional energy and put everyone on their guard? What traits define them?
3) When was the last time you had the chance to really acknowledge someone? Did you do it? If so, how did they respond?

Each day, at each intersection, and in each interaction, the choice is yours to add or subtract from another individual's sense of happiness, value, and pride. The choice is yours as to how or whether you will connect.

Organize Your Online Presence

In establishing yourself as an expert, there are a handful of relatively simple objectives that you will work to achieve. They are:

1) Create Awareness.
2) Model Leadership.
3) Earn Trust.
4) Strengthen Relationships.
5) Expand Influence.
6) Increase Credibility.
7) Deliver Value.

The degree to which these are developed will correlate with the success that you experience, and the difference that you make in the life of your reader. Your online presence, including social networking and blogging, can assist you with achieving each objective – however, writing and publishing a book can absolutely knock them out of the park.

It is interesting, though, that literally millions of people are using this amazing technology to destroy their chances of achieving each of the seven objectives above.

David Ogilvy, the renowned ad agency executive and oft-quoted *Father of Advertising*, once said, "Never write an advertisement which you wouldn't want your family to read."

Since the mid-1980's, I have used a similar thought process as a foundational principle in deciding what to do, where to go, what to watch, what to read, and how to speak.

When my life revolved around the corporate boardroom, I maintained an open-door policy and enforced a certain expectation that the environment would be safe for women and children. I had skin in the game – being homeschoolers at the time, my wife and daughter were in and around the offices more often than not.

When I had my radio show, my audience *always* included members of my family, my friends, and my closest business and church associates.

And as I deliver speeches, write my blog, and engage in social media, I sometimes necessarily hit on some tough subjects, but my hope and prayer is that it is always done with respect for you and your family and friends – and for mine. I encourage you to do the same.

Use your online activities to enhance your writing

career. Begin now to lay the firm foundation for your published book. And avoid activities, conversations, and associations that could damage your brand before it even gets off the ground.

You see, it turns out that your mom was right. Who you hang with does affect your reputation – even in a virtual world.

Online and off, relationships matter. First, we define our associations, and then our associations define us. With the numbers of potential new friendships and the ease of networking on the web, this requires a little work – relationships always do. But your diligence and professionalism will be rewarded, and your reputation is worth it.

Organize Your Introduction

I'll be the first to admit that there are many things in life I do not know, but here is a simple statement, the truth of which I am absolutely certain:

If you do not have an effective way to approach another person – to introduce yourself and open a conversation – the likelihood of creating a meaningful relationship with that individual is significantly diminished.

And fewer relationships equals fewer opportunities.

With a handful of exceptions, we are compensated in life based on the value we bring to others – the hope we share, the products or services we create or help distribute, the improvements of which we have a part.

What this means is that if you are going to create a brand, if you are going to attract a following, if you are going to impact others, if you are going to sell a ton of books and earn an exceptional income and start living the life you deserve, then you are going to begin connecting with other people.

Simple enough.

But I have personally witnessed this basic truth cause a great deal of anxiety and also procrastination on the part of authors who are just not sure how to get the conversation started.

Have you ever passed up speaking to someone you felt might be a perfect contact, only to kick yourself later after the opportunity was gone? I have.

Have you justified or rationalized that the other person was busy, or that you didn't want to bother them by making small talk that could lead to nowhere? I've done that too.

Have you wanted to reach out to new acquaintances in your social network, but didn't know what to say or how to begin? If so, you're not alone.

And the worst...

Have you ever sat next to someone on an airplane for three hours – elbow to elbow – and not said a word until after you reached your destination? Ugh!

There are several possible factors at work that can cause the type of paralyzing stress that makes one want to turn inward. From a very early age, many of us were taught that we are not to approach strangers, and to some degree, there may be valid safety concerns there.

Others of us have been lectured that it's not right to bother people, especially if we have an agenda or something to sell. The propagators of this theory totally miss the truth that millions of people are actively searching for the solutions, ideas, and relationships that we can provide.

Finally, some of us have been exposed to so many pitches and so much spam that we just don't want to be like those aggressive, in-your-face sellers. And that is reasonable. At each turn in this book, it has been my goal to take that anxiety away from the processes of planning, creating, writing, editing, publishing, and yes, now of connecting.

Please allow me to remove the pressure with a story from my youth.

From the time I was quite young, one of my favorite Scripture verses was one that suggested that we should:

1) ASK, and we'll receive,

2) SEEK, and we'll find,

3) KNOCK, and the door will be opened.

As a kid, I remember thinking it was pretty cool the day I figured out that the first letter of each word – Ask, Seek, Knock – spelled A.S.K.

Hmm… I thought, maybe that's some type of secret code. Maybe this "asking" stuff is really important after all.

Yes, maybe our ability – or inability – to ask insightful questions, of the right people, in the proper manner, with the correct intention, and at the perfect time, can be *the* critical factor between moving our vision ahead, or staying stuck in the same place for what seems an eternity.

Yes, ask and you will receive – I like that.

Now, of course, what that particular verse doesn't say is exactly *what* we'll receive, though I believe I've got that figured out and I'll come back to it in a minute.

First, however, I'd like to share another story.

Many years after this childhood revelation about the importance of asking, another point of view on the same subject burst onto the scene. This one came from a person of influence – a boss – though I *would not* necessarily classify him as a positive influence.

Determined, yes.

Positive, no.

A mentor, never.

With all due respect, this gentleman was a self-admitted "control freak" that entered my world for a year or two as I set off early on a career in selling, and then left as I transitioned to the Executive Suite and all the negotiating and posturing and game-playing that came with that set of responsibilities.

Once, in a training session, I remember him shouting, "YOU MUST ASK QUESTIONS! WHOEVER ASKS THE QUESTIONS IS IN CONTROL! IN BUSINESS AND LIFE, IT'S ALL ABOUT CONTROL!"

Looking back, I suppose it was to him, but I've found that many situations in life are *outside* of our control. I've also observed that most people don't much like to be *under* our control, and most conversations and relationships tend to work better when we *give up* control.

So here's my advice: stop trying to control everything.

Here's another similar case in point:

I was having a conversation with an aspiring young salesperson recently who had just spent a few days and a few hundred dollars learning what he called "the art of selling."

"The whole trick," he said, "is to stay in control of the process. And that means asking questions. You can put 'em in a corner with the right questions."

"So *that's* the trick," said I.

"Yup," he responded. "Ask questions, stay in control, close sales."

Now I must tell you, first and foremost, that I'm not really into tricks, and I *really* disagree with his line of thinking. Not that questions shouldn't be used, but I believe that he totally missed the significance.

While I completely understand the important role of questions in the sales or connection process, I see their usefulness for a very different reason. You see, I don't believe the purpose *is* to stay in control. In fact, I don't even believe it's in the best interests of the salesperson to try to stay in control.

If our goal is to create great relationships with people who become willing, long-term advocates, then we don't sell anything to anyone that they don't *want* to buy. In fact, in the connecting arena, we are absolutely kidding ourselves if we think we are in control at all.

And that statement is just as true whether we are dealing with the CEO in a corporate boardroom, a consumer shopping from the comfort of her own living room, or the new acquaintance that we just friended on Facebook.

Questions are important, to be sure – to clarify, qualify, and build honest rapport.

So back to my original story. If that is all true, then what's all this "ask and you will receive" stuff from the earlier Scripture verse?

Here's what I believe:

Ask, and you will receive... an answer.

Plain and simple.

And that is all we can ask.

Ask a general question, and you will receive a general

answer. Ask an ambiguous question, and you will receive an ambiguous answer. Ask a clear and specific question, and you will receive a clear and specific answer.

In any new connection or interaction – business or otherwise – we ask questions that allow us to determine what, if any, potential relationship exists.

Is this person a potential fit in any area of my life? Are they someone who is interested in the same hobbies or issues? Do they have similar hot-buttons? Were they raised with the same core principles? Can I invite them to an upcoming event – maybe to my church? Are they an ideal reader for my book? Do I trust them? Do they trust me?

Clarify, qualify and build honest rapport… that's it.

Whatever we don't know, we ask.

We clarify their priorities, experiences, buying habits, thought processes and preferences. We clarify their comfort levels, goals, current relationships, timetables and expectations. We clarify the next step… who needs what… who's doing what… and who's paying for what.

Yes, we clarify all of the unknowns so that agreement can be reached… even if that agreement means that we're not right for each other and we agree to part as friends.

And when you're okay with walking away, you're free to connect without pressure to be anyone but yourself.

So what can all this connection achieve? What rewards are available for you now?

The answers are right around the corner.

Part 3
Motivation

Chapter 6

Influence And Credibility

*"Nobody need wait a single moment before
starting to improve the world."*
- Anne Frank

Okay, it's time to talk about some of the payoffs. Yes, I know that you love to write. Yes, I've been told that you find it therapeutic. Yes, you say that you'd do it even if there were *no* rewards whatsoever.

Now here's the truth: there are *abundant* rewards – both financial and otherwise – available for you now!

It's time to start receiving what you've earned. To begin living the life you deserve while making a positive impact in the lives of others. You didn't go through all the things you've gone through, learn all the lessons you've learned, and spend all these years developing your skills, talents, and abilities just to hide them under a bushel or give them all away with no thanks or return.

Here is what I believe:

The rewards that you will receive in life – in terms of finances, recognition, leadership opportunities, and personal fulfillment – increase proportionately with the value that you bring to others, and with the expansion and growth of your influence and credibility. Everything from exceptional pay to multiple streams of income, career advancement, offers to share the stage with extraordinary people in business and charitable work, opportunities to travel with tax benefits or expenses paid, new business deals, and the like, flow from you achieving expert status, expanded influence, and increased credibility in the area of your passion.

Now here is what I know:

Of all the things you can do over the long-term to achieve those objectives, writing and publishing your book may be the quickest, most effective, and powerful way to dramatically expand your influence and increase your credibility on any subject that is at the heart of your desire.

How do you start?

You write and publish your book from whatever happens to be your current and existing level of influence and credibility. As you do, you increase your own knowledge, improve your writing and communication skills, expand your thinking and imagination, and craft your ideas and opinions. Others read it and are moved. They recommend it and advocate for you.

In this way, your completed book gives back, showering you with increased influence and credibility on the subject itself. The very fact that you wrote and are published raises your stature in the eyes of others.

Interestingly, writing and publishing also generally lead to opportunities for public speaking, and to recognition as an expert on whatever topic you've chosen, which even further strengthens this circular process of ever-increasing influence and credibility as you are recognized as a leader and expert on that subject. You use whatever influence and credibility you have to write your book, and your book increases your influence and credibility.

In the mid-to-late-1990's, Rachael Ray was going home. The amazingly popular television personality and bestselling author was suddenly leaving New York City and moving back to her roots in upstate New York.

Of course, at the time, no one knew her as a celebrity, and her first book had not yet been given a thought. No one knew that she would soon break onto the scene, create a powerful and exceptionally profitable brand, and improve the quality of life for several hundreds of thousands of enthusiastic viewers daily.

Today, I know people who determine what *they're* having for dinner, by what *Rachael* is having for dinner!

But in 1997, she was just a young woman who was working hard, doubling as both a buyer and cook for a food company in Albany. According to an enlightening, wide-ranging interview with *The New York Times*, she developed a talent for whipping together home-cooked meals in 30 minutes or less and, as part of a promotion, offered to teach some classes.

People enjoyed them, and she picked up a few spots on local television. But her local audience wanted something more. They wanted something that they could take with them – something that they could read and follow. They wanted a book.

They wouldn't wait long. In July of 1999, she bundled up some of her favorite recipes and had them published in a book called *30-Minute Meals*.

Being seen on the air (public speaking) and being published in print (authorship) is like throwing gasoline on the influence and credibility fire – it is a powerful combination. A public radio station called next, followed by an invitation to discuss her book and her methods on *Today*.

Less than twenty-four hours later, she signed a contract with the Food Network, where she has made a home ever since. By the way, if you're wondering about her first book, as of this writing, it is *still* a bestseller, with a four-star rating on Amazon and Barnes & Noble.

It's really no secret.

As I said earlier, there may be no more effective way to open the floodgates of influence and credibility than to become a published author who possesses the ability to speak in public. It is a powerful key towards gaining a reputation as a recognized authority.

Think of any seminar, expo, or training event that you've ever attended on any subject – career, leisure, home and garden, sports and vacation, hobbies, art, you name it – the experts are those who are either presenting on stage at the front of the room, or those selling books or courses at tables at the back of the room.

This statement is inarguable. We all recognize it as fact and, in our culture, the groundwork for that understanding was laid at a very early age.

From our earliest schooling experiences we accept three groups of people as experts:

1) Parents or other adults who can share personal insights with us (experience).
2) Teachers (public speakers) who use prepared materials (books).
3) The producers of those materials (researchers, authors, and publishers).

At various places throughout this book, I have used terms such as author, expert, writer, leader, and authority almost interchangeably. There are three reasons for this:

1) Making a decision to step out to create or to write and expand on any topic is a leadership quality. By doing so, you are rising from the crowd, calling attention to yourself, and asking your reader to listen to and consider what you have to say. By writing and publishing your book, you are adding to the conversation, bringing to it a point of view that was absent before you arrived. No one can say what *you* say. No one can say it the way *you* say it. And no one can bring *your* personal examples and insights to the table.

2) Writing and publishing your book puts you squarely in the corner with millions of others who are self-employed. Whether or not it is your only source of income and support or whether you work part-time or full-time elsewhere is of little consequence. When you are a creator, you have an abundance of free will. There is no superior to tell you how to write, what to write, when to write, or how much to write. This requires sound judgment and the ability to make decisions. It also requires discipline and willingness to follow through on those decisions. These are also leadership qualities – values, if you will – that will profoundly affect your level of influence and credibility with your reader.

3) I make the link between you as an author and you as a leader because that is exactly what our world needs. It is what your reader is seeking, and what I believe you are. You are not writing just another book. You are not copying another author's work. You are volunteering to get in the game – demanding to get in the game. That is what leaders

do. Your reader is looking for someone whom he or she can follow, someone to mentor them, someone they can count on – someone with positive influence and genuine credibility. I believe you are that person, or you wouldn't be reading *my* book or writing *your* book to begin with.

A Return To Authenticity And Values

A few pages back, I included the story of Rachael Ray, and I did so for one very important reason: it is a story of passion and desire – a passion for food, and a desire to help others. And despite her success, over the years she has faced plenty of criticism from chefs around the world with names you've never heard and faces you'd never recognize if you met them on the street.

When asked by *The New York Times* interviewer about this criticism, she shook it off.

"I never said I was the greatest thing ever. I just think people should be able to cook even if they don't have a bunch of time or money." And as for the comments that she lacks formal training, she was quoted as follows, "I have no formal anything. I'm completely unqualified for any job I've ever had."

Don't you believe it.

Rachael Ray is successful today because she *is* qualified, and she is qualified because she is *successful*. It is the same circular reference that we spoke of a few minutes ago – that you write a book because you have influence and credibility, and you then have greater influence and credibility *because* you wrote the book.

Her passion qualified her – not her education. Her

desire to impact others qualified her – not her degree. Her experience was proof that she could prepare an entire meal quicker than you can run to a fast-food joint, and that was all the credibility she needed!

It proved to be mighty influential and credible indeed.

I want you to really focus on the beauty of this story, because so many aspiring authors – those who, in their heart, deeply desire to write – get hung up on whether or not they are actually qualified. They question whether or not they have the influence, the credibility, or the title and education.

It can be a major stumbling block, but it need not be.

I encourage you to think of Rachael Ray's story the next time you question your credentials for writing. Education or not, training or not, you are certainly more qualified to write about your passion, your ideas, your stories, and your values than is anyone else.

If you don't have a higher education or a few initials to throw behind your name, don't sweat it. A well-written book can deliver the influence and credibility that a college degree never could.

Besides, with an easing of the entrance requirements at many institutions, and an abundance of federal financial aid, the ability to list a college education on the back cover of your book is not nearly as exclusive as it used to be.

We'll cover this in greater detail shortly, but you will likely earn the trust and respect of your reader much easier with your life experience, with your passion, and with your values than you ever will with your schooling. I'm not saying that education has no place in the conversation – because it does. But only if that education is relevant to the book, and if the book is dependent on the education.

For example, if a medical doctor is writing a book about reversing diabetes, she may have a credibility advantage over the office manager who just happens to have a keen interest in the subject due to a family history with the disease. But what if the office manager isn't writing about a clinical issue? What if, instead, she is writing her book about relationships, loyalty, and spiritual and emotional healing? What if she has interviewed thirty-five patients and their families who are all going through similar heartache? She's collected all of the stories, all of the dreams and the memories, and has woven them into a beautiful tapestry of hope, love, and compassion. What then? If the subject has suddenly changed to one of testimony and perseverance and courage and faith, who has the influence and credibility now?

If writing from an occupational point of view, you may run into very specific sets of educational credentials within various industries. However, for the most part, the industry of words – of books and stories and imagination – is an industry of freedom. It's a world where you can dance to your heart's content, and where you're held back only by what you choose to tell yourself.

That said, while it is true that higher education can contribute to raising influence and credibility, it is certainly no guarantee whatsoever.

Need proof? There are exactly 435 members of the U.S. House of Representatives and 100 members of the U.S. Senate. Most hold advanced degrees from prestigious universities, many of them in law. Together with the 9 Justices of the Supreme Court and the sitting President, these individuals compose the most powerful elected group of men and women on the planet.

So the question is: how's their credibility?

Are their words and promises written in stone? What is the trust factor? Taken together as a group, do you believe everything that they're saying? Do you believe that *they* even believe everything that they're saying?

"Credibility" comes from the Latin word "*credo*" – meaning "to believe" or "to trust." It is closely aligned with truth and good character.

This book is by no means a political work and has no agenda left or right, but by all accounts and regardless of party affiliation, the public's trust and faith in the ability of our elected leadership is at historic lows.

More and more people are tuning out what is known as "campaign rhetoric." More and more, with billions of dollars floating around, it seems the campaign never ends. More and more, people distrust the message, and this appears to be based on a matter of principles, of character, and of values.

In Chapter 4, I encouraged you to take inventory of your values and create what I called a *Master Values List* by looking deeply into the qualities, traits, and beliefs that guide your thoughts, actions, and decisions.

These are the deeply-held convictions that allow entire segments of your life to simply run on autopilot. When a challenging situation arises in one of these areas, you don't have to think about it, don't have to mull it over or run it by a friend, neighbor, co-worker, spouse or anyone else. You decide and you act. Such action inevitably increases your credibility, and your credibility expands your influence – every time.

For example, if honesty, kindness, and the Golden Rule are values and principles that guide you, you won't think twice when you suddenly discover a stray purse or wallet at the airport, or when the clerk at the grocery store mistakenly gives you too much change. There is no delay: you do what your values tell you to do.

The summer before last, my daughter and I were preparing to leave for a seven-hour drive to west-central Illinois to attend a large music festival that was taking place in the middle of nowhere. We had originally intended to leave the day before, but other responsibilities precluded those plans.

As the day unfolded, we decided to leave around noon in order to allow some margin and still arrive at the appointed time. With just one more stop to fuel up my Crown Victoria, we would be on the road – or so we thought.

As we pulled up to the pump and I stepped out, the very first thing I saw was a credit card on the ground, belonging to the previous customer – the customer who had just thirty seconds earlier sped out of the driveway and onto the highway.

I suppose I could have just left it there and rationalized that it wasn't my problem – but that never once crossed my mind. I also could have given it to the clerk inside and made it his problem – but I didn't feel that was the best solution either, and certainly not the one I would have preferred if it had happened to me. No – my answer was to physically return it.

It was a corporate credit card, so while I pumped the gas, my daughter used our mobile to go online and locate the company. I knew the general area, and we returned the card to the receptionist at the front desk. Thankfully, it was only a short distance out of our way and we were back to our trip; but the decision to make sure the card got back to its owner without falling into the wrong hands had already been made.

So what does this have to do with your writing and your influence and credibility?

Well, as it turns out – everything.

Over the years, Kathy and I have instilled such values into our family. We talk about the principles and ideas and habits that matter. The credibility comes when words and actions match – when one proves the other.

The reason I suggested in Chapter 4 that you create such a list is because it is easy to write about things that you believe, that you desire, that you are passionate about. It is a simple matter to share stories and memories that bring you joy. It encourages others to allow them to see your struggles, your victories – and even your defeats.

In that chapter, it was suggested that this is a critical step in organizing yourself to write. You want to connect with yourself first – connect with your desire and passion – and then line up your book ideas with the characteristics that are natural to you.

As you create your values list, you define yourself – on paper – maybe for the very first time. It connects your values (yourself) with your actions (your book). And it gives you credibility.

What would have happened to my influence and credibility with my daughter had I just driven away and left the gentleman's credit card at the pump?

We both know the answer.

In Chapter 5, we returned to the subject of creating a *Master Values List* for a different reason. In that section of the book, we were speaking of connecting with other people, an activity which ultimately defines who will be on your team – as a follower, a friend, a reader, and a promoter.

We are free to choose our friends, and a wise person chooses his or her friends *wisely*. In fact, how we choose our friends and who we choose for friends can greatly impact our influence and credibility. If we claim to fervently value x, but we hang with people who obviously value y, it creates a potential conflict – particularly if x and y are in opposition to one another.

But it is a simple matter to connect with people who share common interests, ideas, qualities, and values. Yes, it would seem that your *Master Values List* comes in mighty handy! If you haven't yet taken the time to create it, I encourage you to set the book aside for fifteen minutes and go to http://NewMediaJet.com/inspire to use the simple guide that we have prepared for you.

We began our discussion in this chapter with the role that education may play in creating influence and credibility, and I stated that, as far as your book is concerned, I believe it is only important to the degree that the book itself is dependent upon such credentials.

A similar argument can be made surrounding the influence and credibility that one has because of their past or present work experience, position, or title. We see well-known real estate moguls or financial planners, advertising and marketing executives, CEO's, life coaches, television personalities, and journalists writing books from the perspective of their career experience.

It may be that they are extremely good at what they do. However, let's be clear – it may or may not have anything to do with their desire or passion.

Here's one that does:

My dad's been writing, preaching, and teaching since 1955, the year he was ordained into the ministry. And now that I think about it, I guess he had been involved in the process for some time even before that as a seminary student, having spent his junior year serving a church in Providence, Rhode Island.

From what I understand, he already had an abundance of leadership qualities even then, and certainly enough influence and credibility to persuade one very talented and faithful young lady to spend the rest of her life with him!

I'm happy to report that the woman just mentioned is my mom, and that their marriage has been a rock solid example to countless others ever since, and a special blessing and example for my sister and brothers and me.

Together, they have enormous influence and credibility.

And in his work, my dad is a natural.

His communication and presentation skills are well-known, and were revealed early. In the eighth grade, when his father informed him that he was to grow up to become an attorney, my dad declined.

"I'm going to be a pastor," he said.

And so it is and has been. Of course, as part of his profession he is also an author and speaker, having written, edited, memorized, and delivered a twenty-two minute speech several times a week on average for literally thousands of weeks since.

It's roughly the equivalent of about 10,700,000 words, enough material to fill over two hundred books just with sermon content alone – not to mention the individual studies that he has created during that time on nearly every book of the Scriptures, and topical resources on issues from A to Z. Not surprisingly, since I can easily teach him indie publishing and walk him through it, he has recently begun to compile and prioritize that body of work to begin putting it out in both softcover and Kindle formats.

But I keep planting seeds to take him way beyond that.

Yes, my dad is passionate, and he is also one of those fortunate enough to absolutely love his work. It isn't something he *does* – it's who he *is*. Thankfully for both of them, my mom is cut from the same cloth, and together, they continue to work at their passion daily.

Your own work experience may lend itself to the topic of your book – or it may not. But that's why I've asked you to create your *Master Values List*. You see, very few people are living their dreams and values in their employment situation.

And even those who are – if they are well-rounded people – have many varied interests and activities in which they carry significant influence and credibility. Often, people hear that my dad is in the ministry and that he's writing a book, and they immediately conjure up thoughts of religion and spirituality, and assume *that* must be the content of his writing.

Now, that may be true, but he could just as likely be writing about what it was like to grow up on a farm in the Midwest during The Great Depression, or the effects of WWII on his family as he watched one brother and then another sent to serve his country.

He could be writing about decision points throughout his life and the leadership skills that would have propelled him to the top of any profession he had chosen.

Then there is the travel. Over the years, he and my mom have logged hundreds of thousands of miles as they crisscrossed Europe, the Middle East, Asia, Australia and New Zealand. Together, they could write several volumes just on their expeditions to the American Southwest, or vacations to Florida, Alaska, and Hawaii.

Closer to home, there could be books on parenting skills, grandparenting skills, and picture albums filled with the countless birds and squirrels that are fed with love and consistency in their backyard.

There are charities that they support, time that they volunteer, a rose garden that they enjoy – and games, walks, books, and plays at the theater that have become a regular and meaningful part of their life together.

Either of my parents could write about 101 different values and ideas – and so can you. Yes, they have influence and credibility – and so do you.

This is such an important point to understand, because it is not just your work position and experiences that have given you your influence and credibility. On the contrary, unless your work is the sum and substance of your desire and passion, it may actually be your *weakest* area of influence and credibility.

The key is to connect with yourself – with your values.

I was driving home from Minneapolis some time back and heard a radio news break at the top of the hour. I seem to remember it being a very late hour – but alas, I digress.

The lead story was a report of a super-duper mega-winner in a multi-state lottery who had just stepped forward to identify themselves and claim their prize. When asked whether they would continue with their job, the answer was a *definite no*. When asked what they would do with their money, they were a little more sure – they would get a lot of *things*. But the next question and answer were the ones that got my attention – forget about how they'd spend their money, how would they spend their time? Here, in essence, was the answer:

"I don't know... I just don't know."

Regardless of what you think about lotteries or lottery winners who quit their job without notice, this was a person who was completely separated from their dreams. They had spent so much time and so much energy divorced from their passion that a hundred million dollars couldn't buy them the freedom to pursue what they really desired – because they didn't remember what it was.

If you received one hundred million dollars tomorrow, what would you do? Who would you help? What unbelievably amazing life goal could you move forward, and would you *really* do it?

Connect with your values.

The Influence And Credibility Circle

Just a few hours ago, you picked up this book for the very first time and, in the introductory chapter, read the following words:

"...as we write, we connect. As we write, we give. Then we write and connect and give some more. And as our seeds are planted, we know that one day the benefits that others have enjoyed through our work and our writing will return to us as well. Eventually, on this earth... planting time leads to harvest time – every time."

Life is circular. One season comes, one season goes. And then, soon enough, another is there to take its place. And planting time always leads to a harvest.

As we begin to deeply connect – first with ourselves, then with others, then with our world – we get stronger and stronger, raising our level of influence and credibility, and the process of connecting becomes easier and easier.

Recently while advising a potential author, I was asked *the* question – where to begin? My advice was simple, as it has been for you today. Start by taking your own inventory, then use that information to connect with others. And when you're really not sure where to begin, start by writing something that will help someone else. These things always have a way of coming back around.

However, depending on the load we're carrying, it isn't always so simple to connect with others at the start. That was the case as I spoke with the writer I mentioned a moment ago.

"Sometimes it's just easier to be alone," she said. "Relationships were never my strong suit... I'm just not a people-person."

Looking into her middle-aged eyes, I saw the emptiness and understood the emotions. At various times, they have been my own. Yes, I sensed the hurt, the pain and the loneliness that accompanied her sentiments. It is the same hurt and pain and loneliness that proved the falsehood of her statements, because, deep down, I believe that we are *all* people-people – or, at least, we all want to be.

It is said that nature abhors a vacuum.

Now, I'm no physics expert (as my daughter will confirm), but I do know that there are holes in our lives that need to be filled – the biggest of which are relational.

And fill them we will!

Yes, our need for meaningful spiritual and social relationships *will* be addressed, one way or another. If we're healthy, we do that positively through activities that build our relationships with our Creator and the Created. This is a place of meaningful connections with others, and endless energy and creativity.

But if we're unhealthy, who knows?

A deficit in our ability to connect with others leaves a huge void, and given the right set of circumstances there is no telling what we might be willing to stuff into those holes to quell that pain. Food, sex, isolation, cutting, drink, drugs, work, exercise, rebellion, religion, celebrity, ambition, sports, anger, despair, sadness, guilt, blame...

As we spoke, she began to pinpoint a few of the triggers that had been stopping her from pursuing her passion. She also began to identify several of her absolute values – qualities that she hadn't considered in a very long time. I suggested that she use the resource guide – the *Master Values List* at http://NewMediaJet.com/inspire – to help her identify a few more.

We weren't even done talking and she had already outlined four parts to her first book. Forty-eight hours later, she had the chapters ready to go! She was inspired and creating, looking to the future with enthusiasm. "I can write about this subject!" she exclaimed. "People listen to me – I've lived it." She no more than made the decision to write and to connect from the heart, and she was already receiving back positive energy and a greater peace of mind.

And the additional influence and credibility will be forthcoming – we'll send out a link to our mailing list when her book is published.

Of course, your story needn't be so heavy or dark as it was for the author that I just mentioned. Expanded influence and increased credibility are there for the taking for anyone who is willing to take the position of a leader and expert on *any* issue.

As you look to your *Master Values List*, you will likely become aware of scores of beliefs, ideas, and qualities which give you instant influence and credibility on a wide range of subjects which hold your imagination, passion and desire.

I think of Julie, a former business owner, child care worker, and musician who is currently about to graduate from college with a degree in Psychology and Family Counseling. That is her training and education, but her specialty – her passion – is creating the most extraordinary wedding cakes!

What are the chances that she could have been published 30 years ago? Who would have even taken notice? Yet today, she's writing – and in the future, she will be a published author who "wrote the book on wedding cakes." At that point, the right picture on the right page of Facebook could land her a set of round-trip tickets and first class accommodations at a beautiful resort in Dreamland. All because she is pursuing her desire, and raising her head above the crowd.

There are umpteen wedding cake designers you can choose from for your family's big celebration. All things being equal, you'll most likely choose the one that *wrote the book*.

Planting time, harvest time. Write the book because you possess influence and credibility, and you increase your influence and credibility because you wrote the book.

Then there's Katie, who spent thirty-five years illustrating her emotions with pen and ink – capturing and logging every thought in beautiful poetry. During that time, she also raised herself, then raised her family. She worked in retail and restaurants, small business and marketing. She's a faithful wife, a loving mother, a talented artist, and loyal friend.

But right now, it is all centered on the poems and the dreams and the vision that those words represent – for her and for others. She has influence and credibility, and the trust and respect of everyone she meets.

Her book will increase her influence and credibility and open doors for interviews. The interviews will pave the way toward the connections that are necessary to start a 501(c)(3) charitable foundation to help women and children, which is her vision, her desire, her dream, and her passion.

To really bring the point home, I'd like you to meet my friend, Bill. After thirty years in the public school system and some very wise investments, he left his state job to follow his vision. He may have switched subjects, but he certainly didn't give up teaching. Up early every day, he works his passion, operating a retail stamp collecting business that he's owned for decades.

He has major influence and credibility within his market. His customers and fellow collectors and traders hold him in the highest esteem and bank on his advice and expertise.

I've suggested that he should write a book – many think he already has. And maybe after he sees his name here he'll consider again. "Steve," he said, "there are probably only 10,000 people who might be interested in such a thing."

Well, I just used my Google Keyword Tool and looked up the word *Philatelics* – the formal name for stamp collecting – and found that it was being searched 110,000 times a month. And there's another 74,000 searches a month for the two-word phrase *Stamp Collecting,* which would likely be the search conducted by a novice – just the sort of person who would be thrilled to receive Bill's expert advice.

Are you beginning to see the picture? You are not alone, and a good share of people out there are not only willing, but are eager to learn from you. Especially if you have a book, and they don't.

From dog training to kite-flying, gardening to real estate, photography to football, and music to fitness and nutrition! You can write short stories, you can write long stories, you can write love stories. Pop culture or poetry, magic or motorcycles, the list is as long and as wide as your imagination!

Choose your subject, and let's get writing!

Chapter 7

Time And Financial Freedom

"Books were my pass to personal freedom."
- Oprah Winfrey

If you had to do it all over again, what would you change? This was the question that was raised in a discussion with several acquaintances whom I hadn't seen in a number of years. One by one, each stepped up. One by one, each stuck out his chest. One by one, each revealed that if it were theirs to do all over again, they wouldn't change a thing.

Absolutely *nothing*. How interesting, I thought.

Then it was my turn. Oh my – if I could go back in time, knowing what I know today, what fantastic changes I would make! And oh, what trouble I would avoid! Different choices – different outcomes – and a much greater circle of influence and impact! One thing is certain – if I could do everything over again, there are at least a few improvements that I would seek. Here are four important thoughts:

1) Had I known the power of the principles of influence and credibility earlier, I would have invested in them more, and sooner.

2) Had I had the ability, the knowledge, and the technology to write and publish years ago, I absolutely would have done it.

3) While I cannot go back in time and start over using today's wisdom, I can package that wisdom and make it available for the benefit of others.

4) Though we can't be blamed for what we didn't know in the past, I believe that we are definitely responsible for taking what we know now and creating a better future – for both ourselves and others.

Occasionally, as I find people who are stuck, I try to pinpoint what they're thinking – where they're at in their heads. I ask them to describe their perfect life. Initially, it is often a conversation that people cannot even have – a place they cannot go. They have spent so many years having cold water poured on their dreams – by themselves and others – that there is no longer even a recognizable spark left in the ashes of their heart.

The most simple questions can be met with resistance:

How would you like to take a month off of housework or yard work? When is the last time you flew first class or stayed in a five-star hotel? How would it feel to have exquisite and healthy meals prepared for you twice a week?

Many people, when first approached in this manner, will immediately reject them. "Those things aren't important, and besides... they're too expensive," they say. "After all, I would never pay someone to clean my house or do my laundry. An airplane seat is an airplane seat and a hotel bed is a hotel bed. And meals, well... I just stop for fast food when I don't want to cook."

Maybe you've met people in this position. Yet, if they came home from work thoroughly exhausted, only to find that their children had cleaned up *everything*, they would be exhilarated! If they learned that they had just won first class tickets and an all-expense-paid five-star vacation, they would jump at the opportunity to refresh and recharge. And if every restaurant in town agreed to home-deliver *anything* on the menu for the price of a "#1 Unhealthy Express Meal," they'd never eat fast food again.

The truth is that when people can let down their guard, when they can reconnect with their dreams and their values, when they can believe just enough to begin designing their life once again, you'll find that – given the opportunity – they would change all sorts of things!

If you went to work on Monday morning and were given the ability to set your own hours, designate your own responsibilities, and set your own pay – what changes would you make? If you could change any processes that would serve your customers or your family better, or that would improve working or living conditions, would you make them or leave everything exactly the same?

If you could take six months off to travel anywhere, experience another culture, learn a language, go back to school or start a business, would you be interested? If you could live anywhere for the same rent or mortgage that you're currently paying, or put an addition onto your home or remodel it for free, do you have ideas that would work better for you and your loved ones? If all cars cost exactly the same amount, would there be something else parked in your driveway or garage? If you could write a check to any charity today for ten thousand dollars, who would be the beneficiary, and why is that cause important to you?

And we're just barely scratching the surface here, because the real truth is that it is all about the time, *not* about the money.

Time Is Money

In 1748, Benjamin Franklin wrote a letter to a friend who was identified only by the initials, A. B. It was entitled, *Advice to a Young Tradesman, Written by an Old One*, and, interestingly enough, its purpose was to pass along some sage wisdom and help a young contemporary avoid pitfalls and secure for himself a decent financial future. Yes, it was his way of going back in time to help another.

Over the years, Franklin became known as a successful politician, diplomat, businessman, musician, inventor, writer and publisher. And he knew, as we do today, that the right book in the right hands – the right knowledge applied by the right person – could change the world.

Advice to a Young Tradesman is an interesting piece, and it coined a three-word phrase, *Time is Money,* that has been remembered and memorialized ever since. Succinct and powerful, it was passed around the world long before the digital age.

And, like many great historical documents (including Lincoln's Gettysburg Address and FDR's "Day of Infamy" speech), it can be read in less than five minutes.

For your viewing pleasure, *Advice...* has been uploaded at http://NewMediaJet.com/inspire in its entirety. I will reprint just the salutation and the first few sentences here:

To my Friend A. B.
As you have desired it of me, I write the following Hints,
which have been of Service to me, and may, if observed,
be so to you. Remember that TIME is Money...

His short letter goes on to reveal his insights on those two topics – time and money – as well as credit, creditors, property, wealth, hard work, frugality, self-control, and good character, among others.

But it is best remembered for, "*TIME is Money*."

Now, here are a few questions that I have for you, and that I have asked hundreds of people over the years. What does that phrase mean to you? What is your time worth? More to the point, what are *you* worth?

Think about that for a minute and write down your answers. To date, I have had roughly 14,000 employees in the companies that I have owned. Of those, I personally hired about 2,500. At some point during the interview, I often tried to learn what inspired the person that was seated across the desk or conference table. Their resume or application told parts of their story – at least the parts that they wanted to be told.

I was often interested in what was missing.

Yes, it was great that they listed their work history for as far back as they could remember, and their education all the way back to preschool, but I wanted to know what drove them, what got them to the place where they were now, where they saw themselves headed, and, most importantly, where they *really* wanted to be.

In hiring those 2,500 people, I suspect I spoke with somewhere between 50,000-60,000 applicants by telephone, and personally engaged in about 17,500 face-to-face interviews. Of all those conversations, the most memorable are those that revealed the story behind the story, the life and experiences beyond the application or resume, and the dreams that had been deeply buried in many of these individuals for years.

At some point, I would get to the type of work that they were seeking and what they wanted to be paid. In 98% of the cases, they would tell me that they wanted to keep doing the same type of work which they had been doing, and for about the same level of pay.

I would then ask them what they thought they were worth, and I usually received the same answer. In most cases, these were people living right up to or just beyond their means, doing a job that had them much more excited on Friday than they were on Monday, and yet they said that they just wanted more of the same.

In their minds, they were worth what a job paid. If that was $30,000 a year, then they figured they were worth about $15 an hour. Or if it was $60,000 a year, then $30 an hour.

Yes, time is money. And their time was worth money, too... but only what *someone else* said it was worth.

Time Is Potential Money

Occasionally, as these discussions were taking place, I'd see the light bulb go on - it was a thing of beauty. Suddenly, they'd realize that they had an asset, called time, that they could invest in whatever they could trade that asset for in return.

Up until that point, they had been investing in what they considered a sure bet - or at least a safe one. Show up for work, put in the time, and receive a stable and predictable return on investment - x dollars per hour invested.

It's what most people are doing.

However, every choice that we make in life contains both the seeds of potential benefit, and also of *opportunity cost.* We all understand the benefits – many don't understand the costs.

In simple terms, opportunity cost is the opportunity lost because investing your time, energy, and resources in one pursuit generally means that the same time, energy, and resources are not available to pursue something else.

Please note that this could be financial, but it's certainly not confined there. For example, it's true that the opportunity cost of taking a particular position could preclude you from taking another with different potential.

However, for a young mother, the opportunity cost of taking any position may be that she must allow someone else to raise her child. Here the emotional opportunity cost of missing all of the child's "firsts" – first tooth, first steps, first words, first, first, first – must be weighed against the financial opportunity cost associated with full-time parenting.

It is values-based and priority-based.

The opportunity cost of watching television all night long may be a book that never gets written and published, and that cost could be very great indeed.

Many years ago, someone told me that it was nearly impossible to have both time and money. His point was that if someone had a significant amount of time on their hands, they likely didn't have much money.

Similarly, if they were swimming in cash, they were probably working like crazy and wouldn't have much time.

The other side of the story is that this individual happened to be advocating a leveraged business model and suggested the desired outcome was to become profoundly wealthy with scarcely any time commitment whatsoever. Spend your life on the beach, he said.

Looking back, I have two thoughts:
1) Enough years have transpired for me to discern that his model was not a success, neither for him nor for those he brought on board with him.
2) I understand the seduction of wanting something for nothing, but disagree in principle.

Time Is Freedom

Let me begin by saying that I acknowledge that a certain percentage of the population is driven primarily by the accumulation of money and things. I also understand that some people are sufficiently lazy.

I am not one of them, and neither are you.

I also believe, based on my own experience and observation, that these folks are definitely in the minority, for I believe that it is not just time or money or both that most of us seek. In my opinion, the good life – the great life – begins with becoming worry-free, and getting out from under physical, financial and emotional stress. More importantly, it is a life dominated by passion and purpose. This does not require a void of activity, but rather the ability to have some control over how the time is invested.

We want more time so that we may do the things we enjoy or find important. Most entrepreneurs, most small business owners – most writers – are not consumed with the clock when performing their work or doing their craft.

As I am writing this today, it happens to be a Saturday. I have been at my computer for about ten hours and will likely be plunking away for another hour or so.

I'm not really counting, but I already have eighty-plus hours in this week, and I'll be producing again tomorrow.

It's hard to call this work – it is a work of love, and that's where it comes full-circle to you. I can't wait to have you complete this book – to have you share it with others, and to apply the principles to achieve your deepest desire!

I want you to live your passion and invest your time into activities that generate the kind of income with which you can buy even more time!

You invest what you want in return. You plant what you want to harvest. A farmer who wants corn plants corn. It is another circular reference. And one kernel planted, if it grows, doesn't yield a new kernel – it yields one ear with hundreds of kernels.

The same principle works across the other facets of your life. If you want better health, you invest in exercise and quality nutrition. If you want love and understanding, you invest love and understanding into your relationships with others. If you want money, you invest money. And if you want time, you invest time. You invest into activities that have a tangible return – a return with which you purchase control of time.

Now here is the secret for every aspiring author: you currently have *all* of the assets that you require to succeed. Even if you are stone-cold broke, you have the ability to get your works written and published.

You already know enough to write from your heart, and now you can easily and inexpensively learn the steps to publish and distribute your softcover books and Kindle and Nook eBooks through Amazon.com, BarnesAndNoble.com, and other quality national booksellers and online outlets. Get the details at http://NewMediaJet.com/publish.

Excited? Well, I should think so – you have *time!*

The beautiful part of getting started is that the entire

process can fit into the cracks of your life. You don't have to leave your job to begin writing.

How are you investing your evenings – the time you control between work one day and work the next? How did you invest last weekend – the time available between work on Friday and work on Monday? This is the freedom that you currently possess. Right now, you have the freedom to choose how to invest the greatest asset you have – your time. Time can make you money, and money can buy you time.

How? As you invest your between-work time on planning your future, actively writing your book, and opening doors of opportunity, it is possible for you to replace your job income with self-employment income. This alone could buy you 40-60 hours a week to invest as you choose. But there's more. Think also about just a few of those lifestyle questions from the beginning of the chapter.

With the additional income, why don't you let someone help with the housework and yard work? Just a few hundred dollars goes a long way toward refreshing your mind.

It is another circular reference.

You invest some non-work time into creating your book. The book opens income opportunities, some of which you invest to buy some time to create even more.

You *can* do this! In fact, as an author, as a leader, as an entrepreneur, you *must* do this. You must invest your time.

Time Is Life

When it comes right down to it, time is life – and life is time. Life is just time stacked upon time stacked upon time, and when your time is up – so are you.

It is a little misleading to speak about buying time, because that's not really what we do. We have 60 seconds every minute, 60 minutes every hour, 24 hours a day. 168 hours a week for x number of years... period.

What we are doing by investing additional hours in profitable projects is that we are buying the freedom to invest time as we choose. Control of time is freedom to choose – freedom to live and work as we see fit.

Clearly, in the scheme of life, time trumps money.

If you knew that your life was coming to an end, how much money would you give for an extra few years, months, or even days? Answer: you'd give it all.

Because what we really want is time – time *is* life.

But we cannot reorder our time and our life without the financial resources to do so.

Making Money

I am often asked about the potential profitability of writing. Aspiring writers have heard all the stories of those fortunate few who suddenly arrived – commanding mega-contracts, seemingly endless promotion, and substantial signing bonuses or advances.

You and I have heard the stories too.

We've seen celebrities and politicians expand their brands and their earnings by writing their memoirs and tell-alls. These works often receive much acclaim and a flood of presale attention, virtually assuring that the book will debut on the bestseller lists.

From time to time we learn of apparent overnight successes – those who write a short story that turns into a novel that becomes a series, a movie, a television pilot. The process transforms the author into the literary equivalent of a rock star.

At the same time, we've also seen the other side – friends, co-workers or family members who have invested considerable time, and expended significant emotional expense and energy – all for evidently little or no return.

Maybe you are even struggling yourself, playing your ideas over and over in your mind, yet never committing them to keyboard or paper. The questions mount.

Could I ever write and publish?

Could I learn the process and the marketing?

Could I sell enough copies to make a living?

Just how many would I *have* to sell, anyway?

The most natural thing in the world to do at this point is for you to get a little bit of information, grab a calculator, and well... start calculating away!

It is an interesting exercise, but if you stop there you'll leave your fortune on the table. The questions keep coming:

How should I price my book?

If the book sells for x, what is my royalty?

If my royalty is y, how many must I sell to earn z?

Simple math – x, y, and z.

It is very practical, and people cannot be blamed for getting stuck here – it is how they're taught to think. If I want to earn $30,000 and I receive an $8 royalty per book, I must sell 3,750 units this year.

Now, whether this number seems fairly attainable or absolutely insurmountable is completely irrelevant. There are a dozen and one ways to break it down – by sales channel, by demographic, by affiliate or joint venture partner – pick one.

As you divide the task into bite-size pieces, your excitement level is sure to rise. Try this:

There are 52 weeks in the year, and 50 states in America. Take the next two weeks to plan your course of action and then launch a targeted campaign into one state per week for the remainder of the year.

Begin with Craigslist, social networks, online forums, blogs, websites, and e-mail marketing campaigns to regionally connect with your reader. These resources are free or just next to it.

Do you believe that your book is valuable enough to sell 75 copies in your entire state? How about your neighboring states? I haven't even read your book and I believe you could achieve that within a half-mile radius of your neighborhood alone!

Download a map or list of the 50 states, and make your plan – Week 1, 2, 3, 4... 49, 50.

Done. 75 books x 50 states = 3,750 books

3,750 books x $8 royalty = (drum roll please...) $30,000

Would you like to earn $45,000 instead? Or $60,000 or more? Here is one solution: do the math. Make a new plan. Go to work. It's not *that* difficult.

Here is another solution: write another book, and reconnect with your previous buyer. If they enjoyed and received value from your first work, they will most likely buy your second. Many will even refer others and do your sales and marketing for you! There is nothing easier and more profitable than repeat or referral business.

In fact, as you begin to sell your books, one of the quickest measures to evaluate the current health, and future potential, of the project is to look at this one simple statistic:

How much of your business last week, last month, and

last quarter came as a result of repeat customers, either through direct purchases or referrals?

That's it. Repeat and referral customers are the lifeblood of any healthy business – including your writing and publishing business. While decent marketing can bring prospects in the door, and an excellent sales process can convert them, real success is achieved when that customer becomes a willing advocate and promoter of your current or future products.

Repeat business is valuable to you for at least three reasons:

1) It is an indicator of your leadership skills, your expert status, and your ability to connect. Repeat customers are a sign that your brand is capable of inspiring trust, and creating the types of experiences and relationships that are the foundation for long-term success.

2) Only repeat customers have the potential to become advocates for you and your brand. Repeat business and referral business are opposite sides of the same coin. They work together as loyal customers spread the word on your behalf. This loyalty, however, can only develop over time.

3) The costs of marketing and sales are dramatically reduced when working with enthusiastic and willing repeat buyers and their referrals. Not only can we eliminate much of the expense of bringing new readers in the door, but the conversion rate on referrals is enormous in comparison to other contacts. And less expense means more left over in your bank account.

Beyond The Book

A moment ago, I made the statement that it is a simple matter to sell your next book to someone who was thrilled with your last one. That is the absolute truth, but it does not go far enough. The fact is that once you have earned the trust of a satisfied reader – when you have influence and credibility – it is a simple matter to sell *any* related product or service to them!

As we have just seen, your book is a powerful tool in increasing your status as an expert and recognized authority. That status brings with it the potential for much more powerful tools – tools that literally open the doors to unbridled opportunity.

How does this work?

Your book, summarized in a few well-written and well-placed press releases, is the fastest route to local radio and television interviews that you have ever seen.

If you're not sure how to write a proper press release, we have created an exceptional template and it's waiting for you at http://NewMediaJet.com/inspire. You can have it for free.

Traditional media outlets are always on the lookout for a good story that they can insert between what is often a steady drip of inflammatory or anxiety-producing reports from around the world.

When events seem crazy and out of control, viewers like to have stability and hope in their own lives, and the news channels are ultimately in the business of satisfying their audience. The story of your success, *Local Author Makes Good*, is a tremendous counterbalance and one that plays to perfection on the early morning shows.

Your book and your story - regardless of the genre - provides the kind of hope, inspiration, and motivation that countless viewers, listeners, and readers search for every morning before starting their day.

Further, traditional media channels like newspapers, television, and radio do not want to be outdone by the non-traditional media channels, such as mobile communications, blogs, websites, podcasting sites, video sharing sites, live and recorded webinars, Internet radio, Quick Response (QR) technology, and the like.

You have virtually unlimited access to getting your message out through the new media channels. As you do, if you will alert the traditional media - with respect and professionalism - you will get their attention.

Public relations (PR) of this nature is powerful, and can be viewed as another form of networking. Remember that one of the main benefits of networking is that the influence and credibility that the other party has with *their* contacts is now bestowed upon you.

For better or worse, the public perceives media coverage of a story or individual as an endorsement or indictment of that story or individual directly - an endorsement, if positive; and indictment, if negative.

A five-minute interview on the morning show or a handful of paragraphs in that magazine or newspaper dramatically raise your status in the eyes of every viewer, listener, and reader who trusts that particular media source.

The significance of this set of dynamics cannot be overstated. Everything begins with the writing of your book, but the book is just the beginning - containing the seeds of influence, of credibility, of visibility, and of whatever product you choose to launch next.

Next product?

Absolutely. You are paving the way to your brilliant future and building a firm foundation for your financial life, as well as the legacy which we will discuss in the next chapter.

If you decided today to build a beautiful, safe, and sustainable home, you would definitely bring with you a hammer. However, you wouldn't bring *only* a hammer – you'd bring all of the tools that were required to achieve your goal with excellence.

Your book becomes the foundation for the entire marketing plan. It separates you from your competition, expands your influence and credibility, and increases your status in the eyes of your reader.

Your book is tangible – something to hold, to ponder, to share. It cuts away the noise and the rhetoric, while attracting a crowd.

More importantly, the creative process as described here organizes your thoughts, your ideas, your stories, and easily separates your material – what belongs in your book, and what doesn't.

Please don't miss what I am about to say next.

Often, there is content that would benefit your customer and significantly improve their value, experience, and results if it were delivered in a format other than print – say, in an audio or video or seminar format instead.

This can be extremely beneficial to your reader, your wider audience, your brand, and your legacy.

For example, in Chapter 4 we spoke of the moment when it became crystal clear that including an entire step-by-step publishing course for softcover and Kindle within this book would have been disastrous to the project.

Teaching a comprehensive course on softcover and Kindle publishing in a print-only format would have been monotonous and cumbersome at best, and uninspiring and discouraging at worst. I can just read the reviews now:

"Bring your pillow – you're in for a *very* long night!"

"As exciting as your high school statistics class!"

"Wait for the movie..."

Exactly – the movie! The video course.

There may have been a time when the only way to have taught such a course outside of a live lecture or seminar environment would have been through the printed page, but that certainly is not the case in *this* century!

Especially when it comes to topics of a teaching or how-to nature, it is much easier to learn by watching and doing than it is by reading and remembering.

It is likely that these new mediums and technologies will be an important component to your abundance and prosperity as well. Here's why: as you begin down this trail, it will become evident that many such products are able to live their entire life cycle in the digital space, created and delivered through new and developing technology.

Once produced, digital products are easily edited and upgraded, and cost next to nothing to store and distribute – adding significantly to your bottom line while reducing cost and investment for your customer. This is truly a thing of beauty!

Where do you want to go from there? The sky is the limit! Remember our earlier conversation and the solution to you earning $30,000 – the one where you would target with great intention the sale of 75 books per state, one state at a time for a year?

Here is an idea just to get you thinking. Please consider this and realize that you are only beginning to scratch the surface: with those 3,750 books that you sell, you might create an e-mail list and begin to search for valuable content related to your reader's passion and desire. You begin to connect, offering a free online *Meet And Greet.* You do it all through a series of free conference calls, and record them for those who couldn't or didn't make it.

You ask questions.

You answer questions.

You connect.

Now would be a good time to begin writing Book #2.

While you're at it, you open a membership site and offer a weekly call to discuss areas of common interest, a monthly newsletter, and an annual contest or reward for whatever makes sense. You price it at $9 per month for the membership, and give away a $4,500 cruise, a few iPads, or five hours of free coaching.

You also create an audio and Kindle version of your book for $9 and $4 respectively, and in-depth audio and video courses for $49 and $197.

What might those numbers look like?

Understanding that this model will build over the course of a year – and continue to grow well into the future – nonetheless, for simplicity's sake, I'll base it on a snapshot encompassing a full 12 months using the following static numbers:

Let's say that you sell those 3,750 softcovers with a royalty of $8 apiece. Assuming you get Book #2 done in a reasonable amount of time, you may likely be able to sell another one-third of that many again (1,250), bringing your total softcover sales to 5,000 (5,000 x $8 royalty).

Also, you need to know that Kindle sales for many authors are running ten to one hundred times that of their softcover sales, but let's assume yours just run even, at a royalty of $2.80. That's an additional 5,000 Kindle sales (5,000 x $2.80).

Out of your total of 10,000 happy and satisfied softcover and Kindle readers, assume that 15% of them are excited enough to go down the road with you on your basic membership (10,000 x 15% x $9 x 12 months).

Let's also assume that half of those purchase an audio course (10,000 x 7.5% x $49), and one-third of the audio buyers purchase a video course (10,000 x 2.5% x $197).

Whew, you didn't know that you were going to get a math lesson or have to work out story problems today, did you! Take heart – I have already solved the equation for you:

5,000 x $8 =	$ 40,000
5,000 x $2.80 =	$ 14,000
10,000 x 15% x $9 x 12 =	$ 162,000
10,000 x 7.5% x $49 =	$ 36,750
10,000 x 2.5% x $197 =	$ 49,250
	$ 302,000

And we haven't even spoken about the consulting gigs or additional revenue from any current business you're doing that will now increase because of your expert status!

Of course, I could be wrong, and you could sell less – what if it were only one half, or one third, or even a fraction of that? How would even one thousand extra dollars every week or two begin to change the environment in your home? What options would it give you?

You may have a ready answer – your priorities all

lined out – but most people don't. It can be a difficult assignment because, until now, there was little hope or belief that such a dream could come true. For that reason, I have uploaded a helpful worksheet called *My Money Plan* to help you with this exercise at http://NewMediaJet.com/inspire.

Take a few minutes now and work through the list. When you have the additional funds, what difference will it make for you? What would have been different in your life today – what plans would you make for tomorrow – if you had the extra time and financial resources?

Now consider this: I stated a moment ago that I could have been wrong in my assumptions and you may sell less units than that example. Even then, it's still pretty good!

But what if I was wrong in the other direction? What if you sell more? The numbers that were used in our original assumptions were based on a one-to-one softcover-to-Kindle ratio. However, what if you are one of those authors whose Kindle sales explode by a factor of ten or one hundred to one? What then?

Your Passion, Your Profession

This is a book about writing. It is also a book about living. It is about writing and living from your passion.

There were several questions I asked in every interview I ever conducted – they had to do with vision. I wanted to know how people had gotten to where they were. I wanted to know what made them decide to do what they were now doing for a living. And I wanted to know where they were headed. What I found is that most people never really evaluate, plan, and execute a strategy to allow them to live their dreams. Worse, as life begins to pile up, as they take on more responsibilities, as they get older and further from their desire, people often fall into thought patterns that rationalize why they couldn't achieve, why they didn't achieve, or why it just wasn't that important in the first place.

But it *is* important – in fact, this side of heaven, finding and fulfilling your purpose here is *everything*. It connects you deeply with others and with yourself.

It is also an area in which I have struggled. Unlike my dad, who saw his future clearly from the time he was a child, my path often did not seem clear to me. I suppose I was fortunate to be open to opportunity and to change, and to have a decent set of communication skills and business sense.

Here is one thing I've learned: when you find yourself working and living your passion, you will find yourself writing and selling your passion.

One of the greatest days in your life is the day you learn that someone is willing to pay you for helping them get better at something you're already good at. In most cases you don't need a degree, don't need a certification or license, and don't need a ton of cash for a marketing budget.

Here are your qualifications:

1) You are better at whatever it is than your reader.
2) You can demonstrate expert status (your newly-published book is proof).
3) You are willing to share your expertise through any or all of the various channels that we've discussed and one hundred more that we haven't.

I think of a conversation that I had with a soon-to-be fifty-year-old man who was struggling in a career that he seriously did not enjoy. The money was decent – however, his passion was last seen sometime around his thirtieth birthday. Not surprisingly, he was struggling in his marriage also, and his wife was stuck in a difficult position where she had long felt unloved, unappreciated, and underemployed.

As we spoke, this gentleman asked me if I really believed that one should only do for work what they truly love in life. Now, if you've read a handful of the articles that I've written on topics such as these, my answer likely will not surprise you.

"Well, only if you really want to live a happy and fulfilled life, reach your true potential, and impact the lives of others," I said. "Otherwise, just go ahead and follow the crowd and kinda fall into whatever comes along. You can float with it for forty-five years or so and see what happens."

I continued, "For sure it'll lead somewhere – just probably not where you'd like it to if you had the choice. Oh, and by the way, you *do* have the choice."

"Yeah," he said, "but wait 'til I tell you my passion..."

He said that he had started flipping houses a number of years ago when the market was good, and had been able to continue profitably, even as the market tightened considerably.

"I love it," he said. "I love everything about it, but..."

Uh-oh, here it comes... *"but"* what?

I tend to cringe whenever I hear it. You know:

I would like to do that, but...

I planned on being there, but...

I wanted to take care of that for you, but...

I appreciate what you did, but...

I really do love you, but...

Ouch.

That one little word, "but," usually changes the entire message. In fact, most often, it literally erases everything that came before it! Now, back to my friend's comments:

"I love flipping houses, it gives me a bit of control and an element of freedom I don't have in my career, *but*... I can only do a couple of transactions per year."

I was interested. "Please continue," I said. "I really want to hear more about your passion."

He went on to explain that, though he was good at it, though he loved it, though he'd found a process to move houses even in a tough market, it was too time-consuming, and therefore his income potential was limited.

He still needed to keep his job, he said – a job which he admitted he didn't like, in which he did not feel appreciated, and which had recently begun to bring stress at levels that were now raising health concerns. In light of those revelations, I asked him about pursuing his dream full-time.

"At this point, I can probably top out with an extra $45,000 a year. It buys some nice toys, *but*... it really just has to stay a hobby right now."

There it was again – "but."

I asked what alternatives he had considered.

"The *only* other thing I could do is hire someone to help manage the projects, *but*... then there goes the profit."

Are you seeing the same pattern here that I am?

Typically, the *buts* are one thing, and are often fairly easy to work with, if we're willing to search for solutions. However, did you catch the other small word that was thrown into his last sentence? I hope so, because it's a real showstopper.

What's troubling is when we quit searching for

answers altogether – when we latch onto a single option like it's the *only* one. Reread my friend's statement: "The *only* other thing I could do is…"

"The *only* other thing…"

"The *only* other thing…"

"The *only* other thing…"

In a world of infinite possibilities, "The *only* other thing…" he could think of was a way to reduce his profit margin to near zero. So I asked him three simple questions:

1) Are you as good at what you do as you say you are?
2) Do you love it as much as you say you do?
3) Are you willing to document your process and share it with others so that they may duplicate your results?

Oh, and then I threw this in for good measure:

4) Can you and your wife work together as a team?

His answers: yes, yes, yes, and absolutely yes! Wow – here we have a couple who possess a system that could help others earn an additional $45,000 per year in a down market! It can be documented and duplicated, put into a book – softcover and Kindle – and used to pave the way for a monthly newsletter and membership site (likely with multiple levels), and audio and video courses of the kind we discussed earlier.

I also suggested that they consider branding themselves as a couple. In a world with so much family instability, this is highly attractive, and working with your loved ones on the same team can be powerful in your finances and your relationships. There is something about winning together consistently that rekindles the fire!

As we spoke, I asked if they had ever considered putting together a weekend seminar – they hadn't. I asked if they were willing to learn how to do it – they were! So I threw out a few numbers:

"Make it three and a half days of intensive training – give them everything. Hold nothing back. Have it in the closest city that has 600,000 people in the metro – let them bring a guest with them, and you pay for their food and their hotel. Throw in a book and the audio and video courses – once produced, they cost next to nothing. Charge $2,495, and you'll clear $1,800."

If just five couples show up, my friends will have a $9,000 weekend. If twenty-five couples attend, they'll net $45,000 – the same as they used to make in an entire year!

And because we have a free enterprise economy, they could easily decide to conduct such a seminar more often – say, once a quarter, or even once a month! You can do the same.

And we haven't even mentioned the advertising revenue that this couple could pull in from support organizations in their industry: real estate agents, mortgage companies, banks, credit unions, insurance companies, appraisers, you name it.

Every one of these peripheral industries is loaded with businesspeople who are looking to attract qualified leads for their products, and the same is true for you and your career or hobby. This model may be followed, with slight alterations, regardless of your passion or your profession – and, by now, I hope you're beginning to see that you *can* make your passion and profession one and the same. It all begins with following your dreams, and writing your book.

Chapter 8

Making A Difference For Others

"Everyone wants to be part of something good."
- Steve Buelow

O n a gorgeous Spring day in 1986, I sat in a meeting one afternoon and scrawled three short and simple sentences onto a folded sheet of paper.

Twenty-four words.

I was young – full of dreams – and everything was new. I was driving a new car, working my way up in a new career, and had just begun a new relationship with Kathy, who within a few years would become my partner in love, life, parenting, missions, charity, health, business, travel – and everything else that matters.

At the time, I had no idea of the significance of committing my thoughts into writing. No idea of the power. I couldn't see what was coming down the road in just a few short months.

The meeting itself was contentious – the business was not doing well. Yet, in spite of the trouble elsewhere in the company, after just a handful of quarters on the job, my sales achievements were near the top – virtually matching those of more seasoned co-workers who had been in the industry, and with the company, for years.

As good as my revenue numbers were, one set of

statistics really stood out – repeat business and referrals from my accounts were off the charts, and the retention stats were amazing.

My clients didn't leave.

As I listened to the arguments around the table, as I thought about possible solutions, I began to dream. Quietly, I was formulating my ideas about why this company was struggling. Evaluating why there was such turnover. Analyzing what could be done to improve customer relations.

I could do this on my own, I thought. This is *Golden Rule* stuff. How could the others not see that the pressure in their corporate relationships was affecting their performance in the field? I wrote my three sentences, folded the sheet twice again, and slipped it into my shirt pocket.

That evening as I prepared for bed, I took out the note I had written earlier – the third sentence leapt from the page:

"Everyone wants to be part of something good."

From this simple thought, and much dedication and hard work by myself and others, an exceptional company was born. From the day of its founding until the day of its sale many years later, Ameristaff USA would directly touch the lives of over fourteen thousand wonderful people and their families.

We would make a difference and an impact, and I would learn a most valuable lesson: when you bless others consistently, in some way you are typically blessed yourself.

It is like a law of nature. Seed time, harvest time. Sowing, reaping. What goes around, comes around – for better or worse.

Don't Settle For Success

Here is a principle that changed my life. I wish I could tell you where I learned it.

It may have been a concept that I heard in one of many sociology or economics courses along the way, though it could just as likely be something I picked up in a sermon somewhere, or learned from my elderly neighbor when I was a kid.

After all, Mr. Andrews was known throughout the neighborhood as knowing a little something about everything, and he regularly gave out advice and life lessons that I assumed he had learned personally from Abe Lincoln or George Washington or Aristotle or someone!

But the idea is this: in societies in general – and within each of our individual lifetimes in particular – people transition from early states of *survival* and *dependence* (in which, unfortunately, some seem content to remain), to eventual *stability* and possible *success*. Around the world today, and certainly in America, this is what most strive to achieve: *success*.

Billboards, television, radio, and other media tout the benefits of working for *this* company over *that,* getting your degree from a specific institution, making one decision over another. All promise to make you more successful – whatever that means.

In fact, the drive to succeed not only permeates our activities, but is also the force behind much of the competition that engulfs our relationships. To illustrate, if you are to succeed in attaining a certain "position" in the corporate world, you must often do it at the expense of someone else failing to attain it.

But here are my questions: is succeeding all there really is, and are *you* settling for success? You see, beyond survival, beyond dependence, after becoming stable and successful, there is a higher place. Yes, a fifth step that few aspire to, and even fewer reach.

It is, in a word – *significance*.

To contrast, success is tied up with the achievement of personal health, wealth, and happiness. It is focused on *you* becoming everything *you* can be, and having all *you* can have. And it often comes wrapped in "status," a game in which the winner acquires things they neither want nor need, with money they do not really have, to impress people they don't even necessarily like.

Yes, success is all about the impact to us and our lives.

Significance, on the other hand, is all about impacting others. American philosopher William James (1842-1910) once said: "The greatest use of one's life, is to spend it for something that will outlast it."

In these few words, and with such simple eloquence, I find my personal definition of significance. It happens when we invest our time and energy – our resources and emotions and experience – to help and encourage and uplift others.

It is evident when we give without thought of receiving, when we invest in those who deserve our resources, and when we put the sincere needs of others ahead of the wants of ourselves.

A life of significance is the cumulative effect of many years of commitment to selfless living, and is reflected in the faces of those who are better off because, in some fashion, big or small, we have touched their lives for the better.

Indeed, *significance* is what gives the concept of success *any* meaning at all.

Leadership

As we speak of significance, I want you to think about what it means to lead – I want you to think about leadership. We've touched on the concept throughout the book, and I know that you are comfortable in that role. If you are a writer, you are a leader. You write, you lead.

In 2003, my wife and I were honored to be invited – along with nine other couples – to spend an entire weekend with one of the world's most renowned leadership experts, Dr. John C. Maxwell. Held at Walt Disney World's four star Swan and Dolphin, we began on Friday evening by getting to know one another at a private dinner reception.

It didn't take long before I heard a phrase that has stuck with me ever since: "Leadership is influence." This is a good definition, and it ties in with your decision to write and publish.

Regardless of your subject matter, the length of your book, or its genre or style, you are writing so that others may read. And as they read your words, your purpose shines through – your reader is inspired, uplifted, encouraged, educated, or entertained. You are writing to have an effect – to influence your reader in one manner or another.

It is important to speak clearly about the topic of leadership, because it is often confused with management. You are *leading* your reader – you are not *managing* your reader.

And I suppose that nowhere is the concept of leadership more often misunderstood than it is in corporate America. I recently ran into the parents of an old friend that I hadn't seen in years. I asked where Joel was living, what he was doing, and how things were going.

Funny the priorities that people have. Other than losing his home, his marriage, his health and his family, they said that he was actually doing quite well! In fact, according to his dad, he had just been promoted to a "position of leadership" within his company, though his mom added softly, "I think all the extra hours and the extensive travel really contributed to the problems." That's nice.

By the way, the title that he bought and paid for with his wife and three children is *Territory Manager.*

Leadership, whether in the home or in your career, cannot be granted by means of a title – it must be earned. Yes, in an employment situation, subordinates can be *forced* to comply with rules, regulations, and orders – in other words, they can be managed.

But their desire to follow – and willingness to be led – is based upon a relationship of trust and loyalty that can never be mandated by a position. Without trust, loyalty, influence, and credibility – there are no followers.

Sustainable leadership is possible because the followers believe that it is in their best interests to follow. This belief is the foundation upon which leadership is built. Neither you nor I will long follow someone in whom we do not believe. This truth is even more pronounced in organizations that are substantially based upon the work of volunteers, such as charities or nonprofits. Interestingly, this is the realm where you and I live as writers and readers. Right this minute, you are a volunteer. There is no mandate that forces you to read this book.

You are reading because – and only because – you believe that it is in your best interests to do so. There is no other reason. And the relationship that you will have with your own reader is the same.

Helping Others: A Legacy Of Giving

Over the years, it is a phrase that I've said at least one hundred times: "There are a lot of ways to make money – far fewer ways to *really* make a difference."

I was wrong. If you've ever heard me say it, I take it back. The truth is that if we are even moderately perceptive and open to the world around us, we don't have to look far to find something that should be fixed – something that *must* be fixed – something that needs... you.

In our homes and businesses, as well as our schools, churches, and government, the opportunity to take responsibility and to influence and improve and make positive contributions – the call for men and women of character to lead – has never been greater.

Our communities, charities, companies, and families need thought leaders who will think passionately, write passionately, speak passionately, work passionately, and give passionately.

They need you.

Suggestion: write down the number one mission or cause that you would like to see advanced at this time. Then ask these questions:

1) Is this cause or concern worthy of my time, creativity, and sacrifice for the next three to five years?

2) How can I begin using my time, writing talents, financial resources, networks, or influence to impact this issue by the end of next month?

3) What tools and resources can I use to connect with one hundred like-minded individuals in the next three months?

Writing from the standpoint of an expert on any cause is powerful, especially if you are a volunteer.

You may want to use your writing just to bring awareness to your favorite cause. You may want to use your writing as the basis for exceptional income and time freedom to donate to your cause. Or you may want to use your standing as a published author to also seek donations and create your own foundation to support your cause.

You may do any or all three – the choice is up to you.

What is your cause? It could be anything! Here's an example:

I have a friend who rescues dogs – Dalmatians.

I have another friend who rescues dogs – Shih Tzus.

I have a third friend who rescues dogs – Labrador Retrievers.

All seemingly the same cause, the rescue of dogs – and all distinct as well. There are so many worthy causes, so many terrific charities within twenty minutes of most homes, that any of us could donate a few hundred thousand dollars and barely make a dent.

A few months ago I was speaking with a friend who is really on fire for her mission in life. Doesn't matter what that mission is – it's hers. Not only is it a reason for her to get out of bed every morning, it's a bona fide purpose for living – a real cause.

But there was one nagging question around an integral piece that needed financing, and she had determined that she should find people to provide seed-money.

So, now what?

She owns an online retail store and wanted to involve customers from that business to help fund her vision.

I suggested that she enlist people into her cause, allow them to learn about the project through her book and related resources, and to support the work by supporting her through purchases of her retail products and through direct donations.

After all, she would only need to bring 30-40 advocates on board who believe in:

1) The value of her book and related products, and

2) The value of the mission she is on.

Shouldn't be too difficult… because all are worth every penny. I spoke with her again last evening, and asked how it was going. "Well," she said, "I guess it's okay, but…"

Remember that the little word "but" usually erases what came before? In this case, that meant that it was *not* going okay.

Since she was behind on her goals for the period, and was right up against the end of the month, I asked if she had communicated with her customers in the past few days.

She said that she had – she had called them all and mentioned how much she'd appreciate their business if, indeed, they had an order. She offered discounts to others as a last-minute incentive, and spoke to each about a new product line coming out in the next few months.

But there was no vision. No talk of the mission. No cause. And she had stopped giving out copies of her book, which laid the entire foundation for her major purpose in life.

As writers, we must remember that people *read* for a reason. And as marketers, we must remember that people *buy* for a reason. If you are Walmart, they *may* be buying your discount. If you are Nike, they *may* be buying your logo. If you are involved in a mission, they are likely buying your cause – one that they also believe in.

In fact, hers is such a great cause that her customers might even be willing to pay a premium for it – but first they must be reminded *why* they are doing it.

So, rather than say, "I'd appreciate it if you'd think about ordering," rephrase it as, "I want you to know that your order this month is going to make it possible for our shelter to do *x*."

See the difference? And then put the book out front: "A percentage of all sales of my new book go to helping *x*... please order today!"

Promoting a cause – leaving a legacy of awareness and giving – is very targeted and inspires the reader who believes and feels and prioritizes in the same way that you do. It allows your reader to become, in effect, a partner in the mission – to be involved emotionally in an activity or purpose of mutual importance.

Helping Others: A Legacy Of Change

Have you ever struggled with change? Most of us have. In fact, if there is any trouble in any area of your life right now, it may be that a resistance to change – a reluctance to seek alternative solutions – is hard at work. There are always options in any circumstance. It doesn't mean that they're all *good* options – but there *are* options.

Now, here is the beautiful piece of the story.

If you can identify potential causes and solutions, if you can face your own resistance to change, if you are willing to do whatever it takes to move beyond the stops and get down the road to your dreams and passions and desires, then you are able to share your story and give your reader *permission* to change.

Permission to change, you ask?

Absolutely. Many times, the secret to taking the first step lies in receiving permission to do so. Often, we are locked into our situation by whatever thought process and decision process we've used in the past. Sometimes we can't see the present and can't envision the future because we are trapped by fear, doubt, and indecision from what we perceive as past failures.

If we stay the course, we can't be blamed. After all, that's the way it has always been. It's the conventional wisdom, and who can argue with that? I want to give you permission to change, so that you may share that legacy with others.

Last week while traveling, I spent some time doing what I suppose many do these days while driving – and no, I don't mean *texting* friends or *reading my Kindle* like I saw someone doing the other day!

On the contrary, I was scanning the AM radio dial for anything talk-related – well, anything talk-related that was also interesting. So it was that I happened upon a Success Principles program that, in a span of several minutes, would lead callers down the path to personal power and significance, or at the very least, in this case, down the road to the local Cliché Festival.

"Get a plan, and get to work..."

"If at first you don't succeed, try, try again..."

"Winners never quit, and quitters never win..."

Now, when someone is struggling, when their plans are not succeeding, when their life and dreams and relationships are seriously spinning out of control, tired one-liners or two minute pep-talks are usually not the answer. No, usually there are deeper reasons for these conditions – conditions which have been going on for a very long time.

If you have experience working through a difficult situation – if you have a story – you *will* have an audience.

And as for the *quitters never win* line, interestingly enough, quitting is often one of the first things we need to do! I am giving you permission.

"Wait… wait… wait," you say. "I heard Thomas Edison failed 10,000 times to create the light bulb, and he never quit!"

Okay, so let's talk about Thomas Edison for a minute – along with another fairly brilliant individual named Albert Einstein.

Thomas Edison is reported to have said something along the lines that he believed that he *did not* fail 10,000 times, but merely succeeded in finding that many ways *not* to do it. In other words, he didn't just try the same thing over and over and over again. And he succeeded precisely because he continuously quit doing what *wasn't* working.

Albert Einstein, who knew a thing or two about successful processes, made similar statements. He is credited with saying that we can't expect to get *out* of a problem by using the same thinking that got us *into* the problem in the first place. And, of course, there's the classic definition – which is also attributed to him – that insanity is "doing the same things, but expecting different results."

You see, Thomas Edison and Albert Einstein understood that when things aren't working, you don't merely plow ahead, put the pedal to the metal, and work even harder at the exact same plan. Instead, we figure out what's working, and we innovate and improve. Likewise, we evaluate what's *not* working, and we discard those ideas and activities.

Yes – we quit doing them. Winners quit doing things that don't work *all the time.* It's a leadership quality.

And the greater the struggle – the more overwhelming the challenge, the loftier the goal – the higher the likelihood that there will be much to quit along the way.

Your reader may have ideas and thoughts, patterns and processes, behaviors and habits – even great and wonderful activities and hobbies – that may need to be sidelined if he or she is to have the time, resources and energy to nail their primary vision. And they may need your permission to do it.

Is the light bulb working? Would Edison and Einstein agree with your plan?

Helping Others: A Legacy Of Encouragement

I want to encourage you to write. And if you're still not sure what to write about, I'll give you a topic now: I want to encourage you to write something that encourages someone else. I want you to believe in someone more than they believe in themselves. And I want you to communicate it through your writing.

The world is full of messages that cause doubt, anxiety and fear. These emotions are traps – paralyzing their victims and keeping them stuck in a place apart from their life's purpose.

Your words and your stories have the power to release them and let them soar. And here is my absolute belief: there will always be a market for you if you become known as a person who believes in and encourages others.

I grew up with a ton of encouragement – it is second nature to me. It may or may not be to you as well, but believing in others, accepting others, and encouraging others are values that you can develop. That said, understand that your reader craves value and acknowledgment on your part. Even at a distance, your words – your book or related products – may be the closest thing to encouragement that they have received in their life for a very long time.

I was speaking with several young guys recently who were seeking advice about going into business for themselves. It will come as little surprise to you that I strongly encouraged them to do so, even if they only started part-time.

I listened intently as they described their vision for their business – and for their lives. Each has a young family, and believe it or not, they would actually like to provide their wife and children with more than what their current position will supply. Imagine that.

As they described their goals and dreams for their families and their finances, I asked three simple questions to help them clarify their choices.

1) What are the chances of achieving those goals and dreams if they stay in their current position? Answer: *zero.*

2) How would they explain to their children someday that they once had an extraordinary opportunity but just didn't pursue it? Answer: *unthinkable.*

3) What was stopping them from beginning this wonderful journey today? Answer: *their fathers.*

Wow, I thought... their dads.

This is the starting point for many who will pick up your book today. They have grown up with alternating expectations. First, unrealistically high – so high, in fact, that they're almost guaranteed to fail. And second, unrealistically low, based on the fact that they failed to meet those previous expectations that were unrealistically high.

Your books have the power to be the inspiration and the encouragement that open a new set of possibilities for your reader. And they will bless you in return.

Helping Others: A Legacy Of Success

I often have people ask me about the "right way" of doing things. It's as though there is this *right* way, and then a whole multitude of *wrong* ways. They don't want to do it *wrong*, and so they plan and evaluate and plan and evaluate and then stress out and plan and evaluate some more. However, in doing so, they fail to *act*.

Your reader will often do the same, and from time to time so may you. I certainly have.

This is a major obstacle to success – especially if you are writing to instruct, educate, or inspire your reader to learn, grow, or achieve – so let me take the pressure off of you so that you may remove it from them.

The truth is that there is no singular right way – there are simply *ways*. Likewise, there are also not many wrong ways – there is just one, and that is to be deceitful or otherwise act in a manner that would cause harm.

So there it is. There is one wrong way to do things, and many other ways of getting them done. Now, certainly there are some routes which are better than others – and there is

218 / Your Time To Shine

likely even a best way – but that is determined by the goals that we have in the beginning.

For example, if I am planning to go to Phoenix, I have many choices. The fastest route from my home would be to fly to Minneapolis and then connect with a flight to Sky Harbor. With today's gasoline prices, that would likely be the least costly option as well. If I were flying alone on business, and had to be there by a set time, it may certainly be my best choice.

But what if I wasn't traveling for business, and what if I wasn't traveling alone? What if I had my family with me? In years past, we also traveled regularly with a sitter for our daughter. At that point, air travel – while still faster – may no longer have the cost-savings advantage, and a better option would be to hit the Interstate.

But consider this: what if I were shooting, writing, and editing a photo book series on historic travel sites in the American Midwest and Southwest? What if the goal were to speak with the locals, experience their culture, engage in conversation, and learn of their history?

Air travel could still be done, though chartering to all the small regional airports would now become extremely expensive, and even the Interstate option would fall to second place as I plotted my course instead on the early highway system of America – the route with the best photo opportunities.

You do what brings success.

The same is true in any endeavor – from travel to health to crafts to hobbies to homemaking to moneymaking and everything in between. And at each step where you have been successful in your life, you have found the secrets that work best for you – the processes and habits that allowed you to achieve in that area. Your reader is waiting. She desires to know what you know – she has a passion to learn, to grow, to improve. And she is willing to pay you to share your secrets of success.

As food for thought, allow me to give you a few of the more popular undertakings that your friends, neighbors, relatives, and co-workers targeted for achievement this year:

1) Lose weight
2) Be more active
3) Stop smoking or drinking
4) Eliminate some other bad habit
5) Get out of debt
6) Volunteer
7) Advance in their career
8) Take up a hobby or craft
9) Remodel or redecorate their home
10) Go back to school
11) Travel
12) Learn another language
13) Make new friends
14) Be a better parent
15) Make better entertainment choices
16) Improve their spiritual life
17) Write a book

Interestingly, in many cases these are the same desires that were targeted by them last year also, and by millions of others *every* year.

So, therein lies a common denominator – and a market of millions. People everywhere wanting to make the same positive changes, and yet they seem to be struggling.

Why is that, and what can be done about it?

Here is my take, and a suggestion to fix it once and for all: our quality of life comes from the strength of our relationships with other people, and I believe that the easiest way to open those doors is to find a way to add value to another person's life – your reader's life.

If you haven't yet begun to write, why not start here? Identify any area in which you have been at least moderately successful. Realize that you can easily connect with someone who would like to experience that same level of success.

Then write your book to *them* – and only to them – just as I am writing *this* book to *you* now.

In analyzing areas of my life in which I felt I attained a degree of success, I believe that there were a few very common threads. I believe you will find your own analysis similar, and your personal review can form the basis for your next book.

In my own estimation, there are scores of qualities that allowed my eventual success – values like determination, perseverance, and hard work.

But these were always subordinate to two others:

1) Clarity
2) Commitment

In every success, I understood clearly where I was going and why, and was deeply committed to and passionate about seeing the result. Clarity and commitment. Out of these two flowed the habits that created the success in every activity in which I've ever achieved.

When I wanted to learn to golf as a child or use a bow and arrow to hit a quarter on a target from forty yards, I clearly envisioned myself succeeding, and was committed to practicing for days and weeks on end to do so.

When I wanted to receive my pilot's license or learn to deliver my message from the front of the room, I clearly envisioned the benefits to myself and others and was committed to overcoming a fear of the unknown, and a fear of public speaking.

When I wanted to start my first business or to get married, raise a family, and become a partner with Kathy in homeschooling our daughter, I clearly envisioned the stability of those decisions and was committed to growing daily.

When I wanted to write and publish books and courses that teach and encourage you to reach for the life, the influence, the credibility, and the rewards that you deserve, I clearly envisioned the outcome of those events and was committed to the process that put these words into your hands.

Helping Others: A Legacy Of Family

My dad came from a family of ten children – three girls and seven boys. Of the ten, he alone is now the keeper of the stories. Not surprisingly, I have asked him to write a book – others have asked as well.

As was common years ago – or at least was common as I remember it – it seemed that there were a number of subjects that didn't get discussed much, and I believe there were many conversations that simply didn't take place around the children. Maybe it was just our family, maybe it was the German heritage – I don't know – but I would really *love* to read that book.

On my dad's side, family gatherings were frequent – nearly weekly – and also unbelievably crowded with aunts, uncles, cousins, second cousins, and in-laws everywhere, in a small farmhouse that is still in the family today.

I never knew my grandfather, as he passed away before I was born. My grandmother, on the other hand, lived a wonderful, long life, though I don't recall *ever* having a one-on-one conversation with her. I do remember that she was a beautiful, kind, gentle, and peaceful woman – always smiling – who, like many of my relatives, tended to confuse my name with that of my younger brother.

I never really understood that, and felt as though they should have gotten it right at least half the time – even if they were just guessing!

On my mom's side, it was a little different.

Being an only child, there wasn't nearly so much competition for my grandparents' attention or affections. Still, her dad was just hitting his stride when he was called home. I was just seven.

In my teens, my mom's mom came to live with us, which I enjoyed a great deal. At the same time, had I known then what I know now, I may have listened more intently to the stories she shared, before her memory became challenged.

I'm going to count on my mom now to write *that* book.

Recently, I met with a friend who owns an automotive dealership in a small town up on Wisconsin's peninsula. It is beautiful country – wine country, if you can believe it, though the residents of California's Napa Valley would likely take issue with that label.

I told him that he needed to write a book.

Of course, I believe that all businesspeople – especially those in small business – should use their book to establish their influence and credibility far beyond that of their competitors. In fact, in this case, the dealership could put a copy of their book – and their expertise and values – in every home in the city for the cost of a weekend's television advertising.

His son, who is now the General Manager and lead marketer, declined.

C'est la vie.

But I pray that it won't stop there.

You see, my friend, Mike – the one who owns the dealership – is an exceptional businessman with high integrity. He possesses tremendous values, is an excellent storyteller, and absolutely loves his grandchildren! He has also struggled with some health issues recently, and *needs* to write a book.

A legacy of family. A legacy of family values.

Imagine the impact that such a work will have on those grandchildren when they're old enough to understand. Old enough to understand the love that grandpa had, to take the time to chart the course, avoid the trouble, and lay the foundation for their success. And the blessing that he will give those children will certainly bless *his* life as well.

Here is a quote from author, Katie B., who feels that she's received more than she's given:

"It is an absolute gift to me to see my words in print and to be able to present my words to other people. But *your* views and *your* ideas are important to someone, too. A story created by you for others to read to their children can be priceless in their lives. But imagine one good book written by you especially for your own child or grandchild – *that* book is worth more than all their other books combined."

Helping Others: A Legacy Of Hope

I once heard a speaker say that in the course of every human life there are two or three absolutely game-changing, life-altering moments that could radically and positively transform that person's existence from the ordinary to the extraordinary.

In every life? Pretty much. At least that's how it was explained to me.

It doesn't matter your race, creed, or economic strata. Nor does it matter if you drive a Porsche or a Plymouth, or live in the suburbs, the inner city, or the plains of the Serengeti. During your span of years, several crossroads will be reached, and the right decisions on your part can change everything.

In those events, there is hope and opportunity.

It is interesting to note that there was one main common denominator in every situation. At the crossroad – in the middle of the opportunity – there was, in one way, shape, or form, another human being.

In many cases, it was merely the work of another individual – a book – detailing experiences that resonated with the reader, offering hope at the very moment it was needed most.

Can you believe it?

People – involved with other people – offering hope and creating opportunity. And what is so exciting is that it is impossible for us to grow without opening the door for others to grow also.

In fact, I can trace every good thing that has happened to me – every grand and glorious opportunity – to my interactions with other people.

My parents, a teacher, a mentor, or preacher. A friend or neighbor, my wife or daughter.

Even total strangers.

I've had bosses who taught me, mentors who challenged me, coaches who drove me beyond anything I thought I could ever accomplish. As I type this tonight, I want to reach out and thank each one personally.

I also want to encourage them to write books of their own – to let them know how technology has changed and how simple it is today to share their knowledge and wisdom and experiences with others who desperately want to know what the expert knows.

And I want to give back, for I know the value that I have received from each of these individuals, and from the countless other authors who have inspired me!

Regardless of the source, the desire and ability and passion that was sown into me by others showed up at each crossroad throughout my life.

"Now, wait a minute, Steve," you say. "You're describing *many* crossroads – *many* opportunities – and the speaker you cited earlier spoke of only two or three game-changers in an entire lifetime."

That is true. And I didn't say that I agreed with all of his statements, because I don't. In fact, I actually believe that opportunity is waiting around virtually *every* corner.

Interestingly, the study quoted in the speaker's presentation concluded that when arriving at the crossroad – at the critical moment of opportunity – over half of all people don't even recognize that that's where they are.

They stand face-to-face with their future – with hope and good fortune – and don't see the possibilities that are in front of them.

More interestingly: of the remainder – of those who recognize the opportunity – most are too afraid to proceed. The solution to their problem, and the answer to their prayer, knocked at the door, and *fear* kept them from answering.

That leaves me wondering…

What is the crossroad of your life right now? What challenges have you overcome, what skills have you perfected, what talents and abilities do you possess that could help another individual today?

What opportunities do you have?

Who and what has come into your world recently to breathe light and life and knowledge, to encourage, uplift, and inspire you to be your best and to do your best – to live your passion, and reach for the dreams and the desires of your heart that you so richly deserve?

And who else is at that same crossroad now? What opportunities could you create for your reader today? What is the number one challenge that you could help them overcome? What joy or entertainment can you offer?

What book will you write, and when will you start?

The Time Is Right, Now

"Everyone here has the sense that right now is one of those moments when we are influencing the future."

- Steve Jobs

I received a call from an old friend a few Fridays ago who wondered, at the very last minute, if *our* family could join *his* for the weekend in Chicago.

John and I hadn't spoken in quite some time, and the last three or four conversations revolved around new events and happenings in his life – not mine – so he was unaware of the numerous irons that I had in the fire.

The timing of his call wasn't good.

Well, actually, the timing was fine – just not for a weekend away. Right now, my passion and my desire is to complete this book for you. I am fully committed to the work and to the results – it is as simple as that.

I am also in the final stages of production on two courses – one, to teach you step-by-step how to publish on and make money with Kindle, and the other to take you click-by-click through the entire process of publishing, marketing, and distributing your softcover through your own author's store, as well as Amazon, Barnes & Noble, and other quality national booksellers.

Kindle is a potential goldmine for you right now, and

it is my desire to see you succeed. If you have a basic manuscript ready to go, you can be up and selling on Kindle in as little as twenty-four hours.

Twenty-four hours.

And your professionally-produced softcover edition, should you also desire to publish and sell in that medium, is little more than a week or two away, if you'd like to walk down that road together. I'll help you and give you everything you require. It is easily affordable, hassle-free, and waiting for you at http://NewMediaJet.com/publish.

Back to my story: when John called, these projects had been months in the works, and I practically had the next three days planned right down to six-minute increments – Illinois wasn't in the cards. He laughed and shot back, "I thought you were retired – you can do whatever you want!"

Now, this is a funny notion, considering my present age. It's even funnier considering that I don't really believe in retirement, especially for me! I have often wondered:

1) Where do people get such ideas?

2) Why are so many people so bent on retiring?

And the answers to those questions lead me to ask *even more* questions: what's the first thing you think when you hear the word *retirement*? Okay, now what's the second thing? Did you say energetic and engaged? How about young, fast, and cutting-edge? Maybe visionary or powerful, athletic, sharp, ambitious, or driven? How about influential or positive impact? When you hear the word "retired," do you think *sizzle* – or sedentary? *Dynamic* – or docile? *Dreamer* – or done?

Merriam-Webster defines "retired" as: *"Withdrawn from one's position or occupation: having concluded one's working or professional career."* In other words, *done.* So there it is – the reason that retirement is not anywhere in my thought process is because I don't *ever* want to be done.

It's amazing how differently people can look at these things. Many look at life from a traditional employee point of view. They work as an architect or an engineer or one of umpteen other job titles, and when someday they're done with that, well... they're done.

When my friend, John, heard that I sold Ameristaff USA a number of years ago, he connected the dots and arrived at the conclusion that *I* was done. Done – as in retired – at forty! The truth is that the only thing I was done with was that particular chapter. It was simply time to turn the page.

My dad retired once, for six days. Six days, back in 1992 – and then he launched into something that he had never done before! He formed a brand-new mission congregation from scratch, and today he is engaged in full-time ministry to a debt-free church with hundreds of members.

As I mentioned earlier in this book, both he and my mom are as healthy, sharp and vibrant as ever. I won't tell you their ages, but my dad was born in 1925 and my mom is six years younger. They believe, as I do, that we should *really* live, as long as we're alive.

Besides, why would anyone quit doing what they really love? Maybe that's it. Maybe the reason why so many are so eager to retire is that they really don't like what they're doing, they aren't living life on purpose, and they're not engaged in nailing any particular mission. Which leads me to ask *another* question: if not, why not?

I ran into an acquaintance at a bank here in town. He works at an ad agency with a friend of mine and, though I don't know him well, he seems like a great guy with a great family. When he asked what I was involved with lately, I mentioned the projects that I am working on – the book for you, the courses for making money with Kindle and softcover publishing – and then explained that, in addition to some private coaching and consulting, I was building a family business online in the health and nutrition field.

"Wow," he said. "Why so many ventures?" I suppose I should have told him that it's because I'm retired!

This is how I see it: why not do what you want to do? Why not live without regret? Here I am in America – maybe that's where you are, too. And in this country, there are no limits to the number of jobs you can have, projects you can take on, or businesses you can open.

Yes, I believe retirement is overrated. If you find yourself looking to be done, maybe it's just time to close a chapter or two – and open a new one. I am going to make several statements now that cannot be denied. Some may try, but they will *never* convince me. Here they are:

First, whatever your age, in retirement or otherwise, you have experience and insights that are valuable to someone. You are the conduit. If you don't make the connection, it is entirely possible that no one else will.

Second, there is no better time than right now to plan for your future – and your future second career.

Third, there is no better way to begin giving back or preparing for that future than to begin writing today.

I've touched on a number of my thoughts about retirement – or should I say about non-retirement – but I'd be remiss if I didn't talk about the financial implications of writing as they relate to your future.

The income component of life never gets too far from our consciousness, so just in case you need another reason to stay in the game – I mean, a reason outside of making an incredible impact, mentoring others, giving back, or furthering important causes... a reason beyond staying sharp, relevant, vibrant and interesting, or just maximizing your mental, emotional, and physical health for the benefit of yourself and those you love... yes, if those just aren't enough... then there's always the money!

Some time back, I read that a large governmental agency was planning to "offer" nearly 150,000 employees the "opportunity" to take an "early retirement."

Similar *offers* have been made to millions of people across the country by agencies and corporations great and small.

Of course, such *offers* are only *offers* if you choose to accept them. If you decline – if you say no – it suddenly goes from being a kindly *offer* to a mandatory release of employment. Being booted into retirement is not generally the preferred method, especially if you didn't see it coming.

From a strictly financial point of view, this type of early retirement – or termination, layoff, downsizing, or whatever they call it – can be fraught with danger. The reason, of course, is that your income stream suddenly dries up, and you begin to live off of the pile that you've hopefully stashed away somewhere. And a lot of piles have gotten significantly smaller over the past number of years.

There are just too many unknowns to put your financial future in the hands of corporate executives, investment brokers, or politicians. As a leader of your family and the leader of your life, who better to trust to put your loved ones, your causes, and your priorities first than you?

You can begin your writing and publishing career today. And if it's your business, it's unlikely that you'll be at the short end of a surprise plant closing some Monday morning down the road.

In a conversation with friends recently, one commented on my belief that everyone should get something going for themselves, and how amazing it would be for more people to capture their passion and leave their legacy in a book.

She asked, "Do you really believe *anyone* can do that?"

Of course, that *was not* what she really wanted to know. At that moment, she did not want to know about *everyone else.* Listening intently, and reading between the lines, I sensed that her question was much more personal than that!

Did I really believe that *she* could do it? *That* was the question that was important.

"Absolutely – no question," I answered. "You're talented, creative, compassionate, and honest. You have a tremendous amount of experience and a great story. I *know* you can."

"Yes," she beamed, "that's true. Thank you."

And as for *your* question, dear reader, yes – I know *you* can, too. I look forward to reading your book... for now it is *your* time to shine!

Thoughts, Credits, And Links

As seen in chapter headings and in other limited capacities, famous quotations have been provided for "illustrative purposes only" under the "fair use" doctrine of copyright law. In most cases, these exist in the public domain. In all cases, good faith has been demonstrated and care has been taken to properly identify the source of those quotations, to represent their original intent fairly, and to credit them accurately.

***

In many cultures throughout history, one's identity – specifically, the meaning of one's name – was closely interrelated with the outcomes that one would experience in life. Often, in fact, before an individual could reasonably expect improved circumstances, they would first be given a new name.

A new name meant a departure from the past – a new identity and a new life filled with grand possibilities. See Genesis 41:40-45 and Daniel 1:3-7.

So important was this concept in Biblical times, that we read stories of God himself changing the names of those He wished to bless – those whom He chose for a special mission or purpose. Several excellent examples can be found in Genesis 17:1-6, Genesis 17:15-16, Genesis 35:9-12 and Matthew 16:17-19.

One last instance of a name change designed to achieve a dramatic result occurred in the life of the Apostle Paul, formerly known as Saul of Tarsus. Originally a persecutor of the new and growing sect of "Christ followers," he later became the faith's staunchest defender. Along the way, in Acts 13:9, he drops the use of the powerful Hebrew name, Saul (named after a king), in favor of the humble Roman name, Paul (or Paulos or Paulus in Greek or Latin), meaning small.

Not only would this name be right in line with Paul's post-conversion view of himself as a servant to all, but it was also likely to be more universally accepted as he traveled outside the Jewish world to Athens and beyond – the targeted audience for his message.

See http://bible.cc/acts/13-9.htm for additional notes and online commentaries. Also, quick web access to any scripture reference is available at http://biblegateway.com.

***

Inspirational links to Ron Heagy's personal biography, as well as contact and media pages and speaking information can be found at Ron's website at http://www.rollonron.com.

***

Jack Welch is a master goal-getter. The achievements and insights that he details from his years at the top of the business world may inspire you to reach for and attain your missions and purposes in your own life. The reference I provided may be found here: Jack Welch, *Winning* (New York: Harper Collins, 2005) pp.15.

***

Walt Disney was – and for many, still is – the dreamer's dreamer. A treasure of his thoughts and insights on family, finances, business, education, art, entertainment, music, and more can be found at: Walt Disney, Dave Smith, *The Quotable Walt Disney* (New York: Disney Editions, 2001) pp. 48.

***

"Early adopters" is a term coined and popularized by Everett Rogers in his 1962 breakthrough work on innovation and its acceptance into society. The original work is: E.M. Rogers, *Diffusion of Innovations* (New York: Free Press, 1962), and the most recent work is: E.M. Rogers, *Diffusion of Innovations, 5th ed.* (New York: Free Press, 2003).

***

A special to *The New York Times* with the dateline, Chicago, *Farmers Use Automobiles* was published March 2, 1901 and resides in the public domain. You may read it online here: http://query.nytimes.com/mem/archive-free/pdf?_r=1&res=9907EEDA1330E132A25751C0A9659C946097D6CF

Upon its publication, this story shocked both the press and the free world. As with many technologies, what begins as a luxury or even a seemingly nonsensical fad ultimately becomes a necessity, transforming the culture in the process.

At various points in the 20th century, we witnessed the shift with cars, radio, television, air travel, and manufacturing technology. In the 21st century, we are experiencing the shifts in medical, communications, and digital technologies that are influencing every area of life that they touch.

As authors and writers, these advancements now offer the opportunity to change our work. And through our work, we can change our world.

***

As editor in chief at *Wired* magazine, as well as former U.S. business editor at *The Economist* and writer for the premier journals, *Science* and *Nature*, Chris Anderson was already at the top of his game and well respected in business, technology, and journalistic circles. In 2005, his definitive work on market niches made him a household name in the multi-trillion-dollar world of marketing.

How do these principles affect you and your money? Read this epic and foundational piece: Chris Anderson, *The Long Tail* (New York: Hyperion Books, 2006).

***

Sales professionals in every industry have advanced their earnings, careers, and personal fulfillment by studying and applying the principles taught by Jeffrey Gitomer. Read more: Jeffrey Gitomer, *The Sales Bible* (New Jersey: John Wiley & Sons, 2003).

***

Is it possible for you, after all these years, to learn and apply proper grammar once and for all? Well hear this: not only is it possible, but it can also be easy, interesting, and yes... even fun! Get the book: Rebecca Elliot, Ph.D., *Painless Grammar* (New York: Barron's Educational Series, 1997).

***

Study the life and work of Seth Godin and you will discover a tremendous example of living one's dream based on focus, passion, commitment, and integrity. Reading his wisdom and insights – as millions do – it quickly becomes apparent that here is an individual who has left behind the ordinary, in pursuit of the extraordinary... an individual who rejected the expectations of others to live his dream. The referenced work is at: Seth Godin, *Small Is the New Big: and 183 Other Riffs, Rants, and Remarkable Business Ideas* (New York: Portfolio, 2006).

***

Combine food, family, and authenticity and you get Rachael Ray. A "natural," Rachael has harnessed energy, honesty, and passion to become one of America's most powerful brands. More about Rachael Ray, her life, her desire, and her journey can be found in this tremendous and inspiring article: Kim Severson, *Being Rachael Ray: How Cool Is That?* (*The New York Times*, October 19, 2005). For further reference (and some terrific dinner inspiration), here's the book that helped to launch her vision: Rachael Ray, *30-Minute Meals* (New York: Lake Isle Press, 1999).

***

Without question, Benjamin Franklin is one of the most fascinating and accomplished personalities in American and British history. Much of his wisdom and many of his insights are as relevant and valid today as when they were first offered in the eighteenth century.

"Time Is Money," the now nearly-universally accepted truth, can be found in this letter to a friend: B. Franklin and D. Hall, *Advice To A Young Tradesman, Written By An Old One* (Philadelphia: New-Printing-Office, 1748).

***

I absolutely love the Merriam-Webster definition of "retired," http://merriam-webster.com/dictionary/retired, especially in light of the fact that the original founder of the company, Noah Webster, published his comprehensive, decades-long work, *An American Dictionary of the English Language*, in 1828 at the age of seventy, and subsequently released his own edition of the Bible, called the Common Version, five years later at the age of seventy-five.

His dedication to the simplification and proper use of the English language has left a legacy from which all writers have benefited ever since. Better yet, Merriam-Webster's basic writing tools are available today at the speed of light – at a cost of zero – as close as your nearest computer or wireless device.

The Author

STEVE BUELOW is a successful husband, homeschool dad, and an author, speaker, entrepreneur, mentor, and coach with the special ability to weave warmth, humor and common sense into powerful messages of faith, inspiration, and action.

In 1989, amid a crushing financial burden and the fallout from a series of rookie mistakes in a start-up company, Steve began to seek out mentors who had also overcome extreme odds and emerged victorious.

He found the wisdom he needed in the books that they wrote, and continues to do so today.

A natural encourager with a passion for seeing others achieve, Steve is convinced that *your* book can be that same powerful force in the life of another. He believes that your insights and stories – your understanding and experience and humor – contain the seeds of empowerment and the sparks of encouragement and inspiration that ignite dreams and desire.

Presently, with a focus on creating relationships and partnerships that excel physically, spiritually, financially, relationally and emotionally, Steve is actively building teams of health- and success-minded men and women as a consultant with one of the fastest-growing nutrition and wellness companies in America.

He is also writing a dozen books, and is involved in several faith-based organizations reaching our nation's youth through positive – and totally rocking – music.

Facebook.com/SteveBuelow

www.ingramcontent.com/pod-product-compliance
Lightning Source LLC
Chambersburg PA
CBHW031924190326
41519CB00007B/409